Essentials of Online Course Design

W9-BXZ-412

In spite of the proliferation of online learning, creating online courses can still evoke a good deal of frustration, negativity, and wariness in those who need to create them. The second edition of *Essentials of Online Course Design* takes a fresh, thoughtfully designed, step-by-step approach to online course development. At its core is a set of standards that are based on best practices in the field of online learning and teaching. Pedagogical, organizational, and visual design principles are presented and modeled throughout the book, and users will quickly learn from the guide's hands-on approach. The course design process begins with the elements of a classroom syllabus that, after a series of guided steps, easily evolve into an online course outline.

The guide's key features include:

- a practical approach informed by theory

- clean interior design that offers straightforward guidance from page one

- clear and jargon-free language

- examples, screenshots, and illustrations to clarify and support the text

- a checklist of online course design standards that readers can use to self-evaluate.

Essentials of Online Course Design serves as a best practice model for designing online courses. After reading this book, readers will find that preparing for online teaching is a satisfying and engaging experience. The core issue is simply good design: pedagogical, organizational, and visual.

Marjorie Vai has been directly involved with online education and training for 25 years. She founded the English Language Studies department and most recently designed and developed the online graduate program in Teaching English at The New School, USA. She is the editor of the Routledge Essentials of Online Learning Series.

Kristen Sosulski is Director of the Center for Innovation in Teaching and Learning and Clinical Associate Professor of Information Systems at New York University, Stern School of Business, USA.

Essentials of Online Learning Series

Series Editor: Marjorie Vai

Essentials of Online Course Design
A Standards-Based Guide

Second Edition

Marjorie Vai and
Kristen Sosulski

Routledge
Taylor & Francis Group

NEW YORK AND LONDON

First published 2016
by Routledge
711 Third Avenue, New York, NY 10017

and by Routledge
2 Park Square, Milton Park, Abingdon, Oxon OX14 4RN

Routledge is an imprint of the Taylor & Francis Group, an informa business

© 2016 Taylor & Francis

The right of Marjorie Vai and Kristen Sosulski to be identified as the authors of this work has been asserted by them in accordance with sections 77 and 78 of the Copyright, Designs and Patents Act 1988.

All rights reserved. No part of this book may be reprinted or reproduced or utilized in any form or by any electronic, mechanical, or other means, now known or hereafter invented, including photocopying and recording, or in any information storage or retrieval system, without permission in writing from the publishers.

Trademark notice: Product or corporate names may be trademarks or registered trademarks, and are used only for identification and explanation without intent to infringe.

Library of Congress Cataloging in Publication Data
Vai, Marjorie.
  Essentials of online course design: a standards-based guide /
  Marjorie Vai and Kristen Sosulski. — 2nd ed.
  pages cm. — (Essentials of online learning series)
  Includes bibliographical references and index.
  1. Web-based instruction — Design — Handbooks, manuals, etc.
  2. Web-based instruction — Design — Standards — Handbooks,
  manuals, etc. 3. Instructional systems — Design — Handbooks,
  manuals, etc. 4. Instructional systems — Design — Standards —
  Handbooks, manuals, etc. I. Sosulski, Kristen. II. Title.
  LB1044.87.V35 2015
  371.33′44678–dc23
  2014048369

ISBN: 978-1-138-78015-6 (hbk)
ISBN: 978-1-138-78016-3 (pbk)
ISBN: 978-1-315-77090-1 (ebk)

Typeset in Helvetica
by Florence Production Ltd, Stoodleigh, Devon, UK

We both want to dedicate
the work we've done in putting this book
and website together to online teachers
everywhere.

Contents

Foreword, from the First Edition

When I pick up a new book in my fields of language education and technology-mediated learning, I am sometimes struck by bad thoughts.

If the book is really good, I wish that I had written it, and I had thought of this new approach to teaching and learning. Thankfully, rare are the books that engender such wicked thoughts.

But this is one of those books.

Essentials of Online Course Design explains how to design, build, and implement online learning solutions, to ensure that learners receive high-quality educational engagement. The book aims to meet the needs of different groups of readers and practitioners who are anxious to learn more about the design of successful online learning courses—and what makes them successful.

As an experienced geek myself, and having spent many years melding the technical and the pedagogical, I have bought many books and attended many courses that purported to explain how online learning worked, and how I should design a course.

In many cases, these offered me technical solutions while ignoring the pedagogical issues. Others gave me pedagogical theory but no support in implementing it in a way that learners could enjoy. Few of them focused on the impact that visual design and user experience would have on the learning process.

That is why this book is so important. I know of no other book that combines a focus on pedagogical learning design and all that entails, with technical background and support, with expert insights into the world of visual design and optimizing the user experience. This provides an added dimension for the online course designer—the melding of key standards of course design but seen from new angles and with added depth and breadth.

The book aims, as the authors state in the Preface, to "model simple and intelligent design and provide abundant examples of good online design." Throughout the book, this is exactly what they do.

One of the beauties of this book is that it can be read and utilized practically and successfully by a wide range of education professionals, not all of whom are geeks or Blackboard experts or devotees of Moodle (or even know what that is).

It is aimed at a broader, nontechnical readership and yet maintains an intellectual discipline that demands much of its readership.

The focus on the practitioner shines through from every page—the inclusion of personal statements from practitioners about how they have learned and taught, along with screenshots and real-world examples of course design in action, help the teacher internalize the skills and competencies needed for successful design.

The book offers practical advice that is, in the words of the authors, "informed by theory but not about theory"—precisely what a professional practitioner needs. It also offers a supporting website where practitioners can find further guidance and resources such as templates.

The book helps teachers move, in Argyris and Schön's terms, from "espoused theory" to "theory in use"—from what we say we believe we should do, to what we actually do.

The authors are uniquely qualified to produce this book. Marjorie Vai has been an innovator in language teaching for many years, and has always been a leader in the application of technology to learning. She published innovative software solutions for language learning long before most publishers and teachers had begun to appreciate the benefits to the learner of a technology-mediated learning resource. Marjorie has designed and implemented a groundbreaking online Master's program in TESOL for The New School in New York (full disclosure: I wrote one of the modules) and launched a new style of learning (and opened new channels of access to that learning) for TESOL professionals globally.

Kristen Sosulski has a solid grounding in online theory and practice, and oversees the online program in one of the most respected universities in the USA.

For me, a crucial focus of the book is how to engage the learner. This is the basis of constructivist learning theory—that learning must be an active process—and at the heart of every successful teacher or trainer's toolkit. Teachers must know how to engage learners, to motivate, involve, and guide them to learning success.

I hope this book helps teachers and course designers worldwide achieve more for their learners and clients. I am certain it will support the raising of standards in online learning across multiple disciplines and academic fields.

Michael Carrier
Director, Strategic Partnerships,
Cambridge English Language Assessment,
University of Cambridge, UK
Former Head of English Language Innovation,
British Council, London, UK

Preface

This book has proven to be useful and popular because it is easy to use, practical, and clearly linked to standards of good online course design. Consequently, there are key features that have not changed. However, this update has allowed us to reflect upon and improve this guide. We have revised the second edition in several ways:

- **Expanded Information.** We have expanded some areas to give readers a sense of what else is possible or how else to build knowledge. We have tried to do this without further complicating the topics. So, for example, in Chapter 3, we have added audio/video to uses of language that before focused primarily on writing. We have also expanded the section on practice exercises to help teachers evaluate how they might best be used.

- **Improved Content.** In general, we have sought to improve the quality throughout the book. It seems that no matter how many times one reads and revises, there are always new ways to improve content and support materials.

- **Technology.** Details and topics have been added, enhanced, or removed to reflect the continual changes in technology.

- **Clarity and Simplicity.** This book claims to elevate clarity and simplicity. We believe that we succeeded in doing this—for the most part—in the first edition. We have edited and re-edited to further clarify and simplify.

- **Better-Designed Illustrations.** The many illustrations and examples in the first edition enhanced understanding and provided real-world models. We have improved the look and design of screenshots by putting them in the context of a real LMS. We thank Instructure, the company behind the Canvas LMS, for helping us with this. (*Note*: Scott Thornbury, one of our featured teachers, actually teaches his course within Canvas at The New School.)

- **Quotes.** We have quoted from some of the best thinkers in the field of online education, as we should. Given the emphasis on design in the guide, we have also quoted great designers. However, we have been very struck by the fact that so many great thinkers from the past have articulated approaches to learning and education that support many of the ideas in the book. It is especially interesting to see that some ideas about education that we imagine are relatively current go back thousands of years!

The Routledge Essentials of Online Learning Series

Learning

It's not about technology, it's about learning.

—Stephen Anspacher

This quote could be the mission statement of this series. Educational innovations, whether technological, pedagogical, philosophical, or sociological, come and go. Too often, we embrace new technologies and approaches to education while missing the point—that it's all about learning—or at least it should be.

Technology itself will not solve our educational shortcomings. For example, buying hundreds of iPads for a school system will not improve things unless we first ask:

- Why?

- How will they improve learning?

- How might they be used?

- Are they better than other alternatives?

- How will the logistics work?

- Is there anything we are missing regarding the relationship of the technology and those who we intend will use it— teachers and students?

All of the books in this online teaching and learning series place learning first. Online learning can be every bit as good as on-site learning provided we keep this focus. The standards we have provided stress this commitment. The rationale for each standard is provided.

Practicality

Teachers need simple, straightforward guidance on how to create an online or blended course so that subject matter remains the central focus of their efforts. They need to understand how to engage students as easily with online teaching as they do in the classroom. The books in the series are hands-on and practical. They are informed by theory, but not about theory.

Simplicity and Design

> For the foreseeable future, complicated technologies will continue to invade our homes and workplaces, thus simplicity is bound to be a growth industry.
>
> —John Maeda

Consumers can usually find an array of easy-to-follow books on computers and technology. Educators have not been so lucky. Simplicity of design helps cut through the technological mire and save time. It opens the mind and pleases the eye.

The series models simple and intelligent design, and provides abundant examples of good online course design.

Order and simplification
are the first steps towards the
mastery of a subject.

Thomas Mann

Introduction to
This Guide

To design is much more than simply to assemble, to order, or
even to edit; it is to add value and meaning, to illuminate, to
simplify, to clarify, to modify, to dignify, to dramatize, to
persuade, and perhaps even to amuse.

Paul Rand—author, graphic designer, teacher

To borrow some words from Paul Rand above, this guide aims
to simplify, to clarify, and to illuminate. We hope you find that
it helps you to do the same in your online course.

i.1   A Unique Guide for Online Course Design

This is the only book on this topic that has all these qualities:

* A clearly outlined set of **online course design standards**
  establishes the core principles. They first appear in context
  then are repeated twice. At the end of each chapter, they
  support the summary and serve as a reflective tool. Lastly,
  they all appear in a standards checklist in Appendix B. This
  list serves as a reflective evaluation tool once the course is
  designed.

* The **guide itself serves as a model** of many of the design
  elements espoused.

* The writing is **concise and clear**, and avoids jargon.

* The content focuses on **practical application informed by
  theory, but not about theory**.

* **Examples and illustrations of good online course
  design** are provided throughout the book and on the
  book's website.

- **Learning abilities and preferences are emphasized** and modeled in examples, and in the way the guide itself is written and designed.

- The book's **website** (www.essentialsofonlinecourse design.com) provides additional reference and resource materials, templates for units, instructions, and models of good online course design. Look for the website icon, at the left, throughout the book.

i.2 Who Are the Guide and Website For?

The guide and website are for those involved with online teaching and training at all levels, including:

- **Higher education teachers/designers** who face the short- or long-term realities of transforming an on-site course into an online or blended course.

- **Trainers** creating online modules or programs.

- **Staff development trainers** who work through the online course-building process with teachers.

- **Massive open online course (MOOC) developers and designers** who work with content experts to design online educational experiences and courses.

- **Instructors teaching about online course design**. The standards-based models and examples reduce the burden on these instructors to provide such resources on their own.

- **Senior trainers to those learning about online pedagogical design**. Again, the standards-based models support the process.

- **Students** in educational technology programs.

- **Decision-makers such as administrators, managers, chief learning officers, and board members** who need to understand technology applications and how they should work so that they can make informed decisions about technology.

- Individuals within an institution, or **entrepreneurs** who work with online course development or training.

- Anyone interested in learning about, or brushing up on, best practices in teaching with technologies.

i.3 What Do Online Students Need?

After years of traditional classroom study, most students have questions about studying online. For those committing to more than one course (e.g. a program or degree), they may have even more questions. Here are some examples:

- How does an online course work?

- How does it compare to classroom study?

- Does it require special technical knowledge?

- Can I get help if I have technical problems?

- Will there be help if I find I have problems with online study?

- Will I feel isolated studying online? Will I miss out on working together with students in a classroom?

- How much of my time will an online course require compared to taking an on-site course?

Teachers should be able to answer the questions outlined above so that students feel confident about the process and its benefits. This book provides the answers and the means of following through on promises made by institutions in their course descriptions and projected outcomes. Standards of good online design are at the core of this process.

For students, signing up for an online course may be easy. Staying on track, managing their time, and being diligent are much more difficult. Give them guidance on how to:

- develop the skills to be a great online student;

- create an online presence;

- apply techniques for interaction and appropriate communication;

- work in groups and individually online;

- understand the technological requirements and how to get technical support; and

- manage their time in an online course.

(Sosulski & Bongiovanni, 2013)

i.4 A Standards-Based Approach

A great deal of work and research has been done to determine what works in an online learning and teaching environment. As a result, standards and best practices have been developed to guide course designers and teachers. Often, such standards are presented in complicated or dense formats. In this guide, the standards are introduced then reinforced in a variety of ways. Finally, they are presented as a checklist that teachers can use to reflectively self-evaluate their online course.

We present standards in three stages:

1. In each chapter as they are covered. At this stage, they look like this:

   ☑ **Content elements are presented in a logical sequence.**

2. Next, all standards covered in a chapter are listed in summary form at the end of the chapter. Use this to review the points covered in the chapter, or as a focused checklist when working through the chapter topic. At this stage, the boxes in front of the standards are open—waiting for you to check them.

   ☐ **Content elements are presented in a logical sequence.**

3. Finally, Appendix B is a standards checklist for you to use when you have developed your course and need to evaluate your work. This also serves as a standards index

so that you can easily find where the standard was covered, and review where and how each was presented. Each standard is followed by the page numbers where it comes up so that you can review as needed. Again, they appear with unchecked boxes.

☐ **Content elements are presented in a logical sequence.**

The reundancy built into this small guide reinforces your understanding of the essentials of good online design.

Underlying Principles

These standards have been culled from a number of resources and our own experiences with online education. They are presented and reinforced in a straightforward and constructive way. Some of the major resources we have used are:

- Chickering, A.W. & Gamson, Z.F. (1987) Seven principles for good practice in undergraduate education. *The American Association for Higher Education Bulletin*, March: 3–7.

- Horton, S. (2006) Design simply. Universal usability: A universal design approach to Web usability. Retrieved from: www.universalusability.com.

- Lynch, P.J. & Horton, S. (2009) *Web Style Guide* (3rd ed.). New Haven, CT: Yale University Press.

- Maeda, J. (2006) *Laws of Simplicity*. Cambridge, MA: MIT Press.

- Mayer, R.E. (2001) *Multimedia Learning*. New York: Cambridge University Press.

- Palloff, R.M. & Pratt, K. (2007) *Building Online Learning Communities*. San Francisco, CA: Jossey-Bass.

- Quality Matters (2013) Inter-institutional quality assurance in online learning. Retrieved from: www.qualitymatters.org.

Note: A full list of sources and references can be found on pages 220–222.

Organization of the Book

The book is organized as follows:

- The **Introduction** provides an overview of the book, with time spent on basic issues, including notes on the terminology used in the book, and a brief description of the website and how it relates to the book.

- Chapter 1, **Orientation to Online Teaching and Learning**, introduces aspects of and priorities for online teaching and learning that may be new to you.

- Chapter 2, **Elements of an Online Course: A Tour**, is an illustrated tour through the elements of a learning management system (LMS), using real examples from an online course.

- Chapters 3 and 4, **Language and Writing Style** and **Visual Design Basics**, cover two elements of effective communication that are not unique to online. Teachers must be aware of the critical importance of adapting these to online.

- Chapters 5, 6, 7, and 8, **Engaging the Online Learner**, **Activities and Tools**, **Resources that Engage**, and **Assessment and Feedback**, cover the essential elements of the presentation and design of the course, such as introducing new knowledge, activities, resources, and assessment.

- Chapters 9 and 10, **Building the Course Foundation** and **Structuring the Course Content**, begin by using the standard elements of a classroom syllabus as a point of departure to create an online syllabus. After a series of guided steps, this evolves into the online course framework with special attention paid to presentation development in Chapter 10, where we again use examples from an online course.

- Appendix A, **Writing Learning Outcomes**, reviews the essential points of writing good learning outcomes.

- Appendix B, **The Standards Checklist**, lists the standards with page references. This can be used as a final checklist to evaluate your online course.

WEB **The accompanying website provides many models of good online design, and additional references and resources.** Adaptable templates help readers to conceptualize and develop the substance of each learning unit. Again, all concepts and elements in this guide are reinforced through models and examples that emphasize online course design standards. The organization of the website mirrors that of the book. So if, for example, you are guided to Web materials in Section 9.2 of the book, you will find them in Section 9.2 of the website.

i.6 How to Use the Guide

Before you begin, scan the book to get clear on the topics and their organization.

Depending upon your time frame and/or what you may already know, you may find one or more topics that you can bypass. If you have taken online courses and are familiar with time considerations and learning management systems, you may want to skip those sections.

A great deal of time and space in this project has been devoted to assembling the models and examples of good course design that appear in the book and on the website. Familiarizing yourself with these examples will strengthen your skills in online course design.

i.7 This Guide as a Model

Standards are modeled in the way this guide is written and designed. The modeling in the guide, of course, is limited to the elements a book and an online course share. Flip through the pages and notice what has been done in the following categories.

Graphic Design

- This is an easily readable typeface.

- Right margins are jagged.

- There is ample space between the lines of text.

- The pages are uncluttered.

- There is a good deal of white space on the page—there is no crowding.

- Bold type is used sparingly for emphasis.

- Graphic design elements are used consistently.

Images, Audio, and Video

- Visual elements are used to improve clarity of presentation and understanding—they enhance rather than distract from learning.

- All elements in images are easily discernible.

- A variety of visual and text elements support different learning abilities or preferences.

Language and Writing Style

- Language is clear, brief, and to the point.

- The tone is relaxed, conversational, and supportive.

- Jargon and technical terms are avoided whenever possible, or defined.

Learning Resources

- An ample number of models and examples are presented.

- A rich collection of links and references to online resources, books, and articles are included in the book and on the website.

- A full list of references is included at the back of the book.

Chapter Structure

- An introduction begins each chapter.

- "Chunking" (i.e. breaking down content into smaller sections than you might normally find in a book) is used to reflect on the breakdown needed when material is presented online.

- Practical resources are included for exploration and expansion of the topic.

- The chapter ends with a list of standards that serves as a summary of core points.

Real-World Examples

WEB

The book and website are rich sources of additional resources, such as:

- the voices of practitioners are included throughout;

- full-color screenshots;

- examples of lessons and activities;

- downloadable templates;

- videos; and

- additional references.

I.8　Terminology

For the sake of consistency, we have used specific words or phrases to represent, in some cases, a variety of possibilities (see the first example below). Once again, we have also done this for the sake of simplicity.

Units

Lessons

Sections

Segments

- **Teacher.** The course designer/developer, instructor, professor, facilitator, or trainer. While phrases such as teacher and facilitator may suggest two approaches that are fairly far apart, this guide does not cover the actual teaching of the course in any detail, and therefore tries to take as neutral a position as possible. Whether we are talking about teaching or the design/development will be made clear from the context.

- **Student.** The individual that is taking the online course (i.e. the trainee, class member, or participant).

- **Learner.** This term is used when we refer to the ways an individual obtains knowledge.

- **Course.** We use this term to cover any of the following: university or college course, high school class, training program, seminar, or workshop.

- **Lesson.** A unit of instruction that distinguishes the different topics within an online course, which the learners cover in a particular order. It can also be called a module or section.

- **Learning management system (LMS).** The LMS is the Web-based software application used to design, develop, teach, and manage online courses. It is usually the virtual environment in which the learner engages with the content, peers, and teacher. It is sometimes called a course management system (CMS).

- **On-site course.** A course that is taught in a physical location where teachers and learners are present in a face-to-face setting.

- **Gender.** We simply use both male and female in our examples and writing.

Chapter 1 Orientation to Online Teaching and Learning

Learn
Knowledge makes everything simpler.
Maeda (2006), 4th law of simplicity

In this chapter, we look at some of the key characteristics of teaching online. Some, such as format and delivery, are unique to teaching online. Others, such as how time is used, the structure of an online class, and communicating without face-to-face contact, require understanding and some adaptation.

Make no mistake about it—your first experience teaching online will require adjustments. The following will most certainly be different from teaching on-site:

- **Absence of a physical teaching space.** You no longer have a physical classroom! This completely changes the way you interact with your students. For example, assignment instructions are usually written, and lectures and presentation of new material must be re-conceived for the online environment. Students will be learning and interacting with the online course on a variety of devices: computers, iPads and other tablets, electronic reading devices such as Kindle, or smartphones. They may be doing this on the go in cars, buses, or trains, and in a variety of places such as coffee shops, home, or work.

- **Online class content.** Ideally, much of this is planned and created before the course begins. This guide walks you through the process.

- **Communicating online rather than in person.** You can't rely on the same nonverbal communication techniques you use in an on-site class. Online, the tone of your writing, expressions of encouragement, and perhaps some audio or video will help learners understand your personality. On a one-on-one level, you will be in contact through emails, video conferencing, or even by phone. You won't be there to clarify points as needed. So, it becomes important to use a writing style that is clear and straightforward. At times, you will clarify by using references to online resources or definitions.

- **Delayed feedback.** It is important to anticipate questions from students ahead of time and articulate the answers within your instructions for activities, assignments, etc.

- **Visual design.** Simple, organized, and clean page design supports clarity and understanding. Using images, and restating or providing examples in audio or video, may help as well.

- **Flexibility.** When you add flexibility, you lose a certain amount of structure. Deadlines now play a key role in providing structure.

- **Time online.** You and the learners will need to adjust to how your time is used. We cover this in detail below.

- **Class participation vs. attending class.** The quantity and quality of online class participation replaces on-site attendance.

- **Office hours.** The way you provide extra help to students and answer questions will change, somewhat. Setting up office hours by phone or text/video/audio chat (e.g. Skype and Google Hangouts) is possible. (*Note*: always be aware of time differences.)

- **Online class discussion and group work.** Student discussions and group work are supported by collaborative tools. The collaborations take place over days, and the interactions, such as comments by students, are recorded for all participants to review and comment on.

1.1 Online Learning Today

According to Marc Prensky, today's learners are not the people our educational system was designed to teach:

> It is now clear that as a result of this ubiquitous (digital) environment and the sheer volume of their interaction with it, today's learners think and process information fundamentally differently from their predecessors . . . we can say with certainty that their thinking patterns have changed . . . Our learners today are all "native speakers" of the digital language of computers, video games and the Internet.
>
> (Prensky, 2001)

In many parts of the world, learners that were 28 or younger at the publication of this book have probably grown up with computers, video games, word processing, and the Internet. They have easy, portable access to the music, art, and entertainment of their liking, as well as at-their-fingertips access to large numbers of people that share their interests or have information they want.

These learners are not the passive recipients of such technology, as their parents might have been. They can and most often prefer to be participants in multiuser environments. They use their imagination and creativity freely and openly. They work, play, and compete with people around the globe. These learners are used to levels of engagement, collaboration, interactivity, access, and instant feedback that could not have been imagined 30 years ago.

And what of the older learners and teachers among us, the "digital immigrants" who were not brought up using the technology, but want to or have to embrace it now? They must adapt. And why not? It's pretty exciting stuff.

We can begin here by becoming familiar with the elements and standards that make for a good online course. Visual, pedagogical, and organizational design need to be clear and engaging enough for all to get it, "natives" and "immigrants" alike.

This guide introduces the pedagogical essentials of modern online course design.

1.2 Asynchronous Learning

Synchronous means that things are happening at the same time. **Asynchronous** means that things are happening at different times.

Real time
is another term
that can be used
for **synchronous**.

If a teacher in New York is teaching an on-site class, or if an online class is being taught in real time, it is happening synchronously, as teacher and learners are communicating within the same time frame. If a teacher in New York is teaching students who come in at different times, either because they are in different geographical areas and/or just come in when it's convenient, they are participating asynchronously.

 to do

Who Are Your Learners?

We can't generalize about who your learners will be.

Let's look at some characteristics of online learners.

Many of your learners will fall into more than one category below. Many of you will have a variety of different students. We hope that this helps you to put yourself in their place and imagine what it's like to be an online student. We also suggest that you take an online course if you have the opportunity and the time, and haven't done so already.

- The "digital pros" are 30 or under. They grew up using the Internet. They are used to scanning web pages, reading short messages on email, text messaging, and using social media websites such as Twitter and Facebook. Digital pros can't conceive of a life without digital media.

- The "digitally evolved" grew up with computers but typically were introduced to the Internet in high school or college. They may or may not find using digital/social media second nature, depending upon their background and attitude.

- The "digital adopters" use computers but are used to reading longer texts, papers, and magazines. They are fairly comfortable with doing the basics on a computer, but may not feel comfortable jumping into a totally digital world with lots of bells and whistles.

- The pre-digital learners may be taking an online class simply because there is no other choice. They know little about computers.

- International learners' first language may not be English. If this is the case, they rely on the fact that the teacher is sensitive to this without being patronizing. Many of you who use this book will have entire classes of learners whose native language is something other than English. The chances are there will be some variation in cultures and first languages in most online classes.

- The classic (young) learners are probably also digital pros. They may be in high school, a community college, or a four-year college. They may still be in the process of developing a writing style. Some may have trouble with grammar structure and use.

- Adult (probably working) learners have neither time nor money to waste. They may or may not be comfortable with the digital world. This group may or may not have difficulties with their writing, and the structure and use of grammar.

Look over this list again. Which of these groups do you belong to? Focus especially on those that are different from you and try to put yourself in their place.

This book focuses on asynchronous learning. This is how it works: The teacher may post material online at 9:00 a.m. on Monday in Toronto. Learners, who may be situated anywhere in the world, can access that material and respond any time, day or night, within a defined number of days.

Asynchronous learning is more flexible than real-time learning since the class is not fixed within a set time period on specific days. Consequently, it is preferred by learners with busy lives, complicated schedules, or burdensome commutes. Learners can participate at a time of day that is convenient. The same, of course, is true for the teacher.

An asynchronous online course follows the daily personal schedule of learner and teacher. Class meets at no particular time and is of no specific length. In fact, an online class doesn't actually meet in the sense that it does on-site. The learners do not need to be online together at any particular time.

Asynchronous online study is really the only convenient possibility for international or global online study because of the time differences. It is ideal for people who travel a lot since they can teach and/or learn on the go.

Asynchronous learning allows for flexibility of:

- **Time.** One can study any time, day or night, within a series of fixed time periods (of days or weeks).

- **Place.** To access the course, one need only be able to access the Internet. Parts of a well-designed course are portable (i.e. downloadable for viewing, printing, listening, or watching when you are offline or accessible on a handheld device). Given the proliferation of smartphones and devices such as electronic tablets, learners can study on the go.

- **Pace.** Learners move through the course within defined time periods at their own pace—up to a point. They move more quickly through areas they know, or that are easy for them. They treat more difficult subjects more deliberately. These possibilities offer learners additional sources of support (once they know about them). For example, they can contact the teacher or technical support because they usually have several days to participate in a particular lesson (see below).

- **Participation.** There is no pressure on learners to respond to comments and questions immediately as there is for an on-site course. **The ability to reflect before responding is one of the benefits of online learning, and should be encouraged.** Once learners have taken other learners' comments into consideration, they may want to or have to (depending on the teacher's specified requirements) respond again. They sense that they are contributing to a knowledge base—bringing in related materials, reconsidering issues, reconstituting the class in a way. This naturally becomes a learning-centered environment. It facilitates the development of higher-level thinking skills. Evaluation and re-evaluation become a core part of the learning process.

In addition to asynchronous and synchronous online formats, there is a third type of format: **blended learning**. This is any combination of at least two of the following: asynchronous online, real-time (synchronous) online, or on-site learning. Synchronous activities can be a good complement to an asynchronous course, circumstances permitting. Consult the second book in this series, *Essentials for Blended Learning: A Standards-Based Guide*, for a focus on what kinds of activities are best used in which environments.

1.3 Online Course Delivery

A learning management system (LMS) can be, and usually is, the program used to create and manage an online course. LMSs such as Canvas, Moodle, or Blackboard (see Figure 1.1) do not require that you be a "techno-wizard." However, computer literacy is a must. You need to know how to use basic programs such as a word processor, spreadsheet, photo manager, and email. Understanding how to properly save, upload, and download files is critical. Of course, it is equally important that you know how to get around on the Internet.

Your institution should, at the very minimum, provide training on how to use the LMS that they have adopted. Keep in mind, however, that these are only the technical basics of building an online course. The larger challenge is the redesign of your on-site teaching practices for effective online teaching and learning.

note

We are not recommending any particular LMS. In fact, you can teach an online course without even using an LMS.

Look at the two screenshots below (see Figure 1.1). The first is a sample of a course screen with the LMS menus visible. In this case, they are to the left of a central rectangle containing the course information. The teacher does not usually have any control over the design of the outer area containing the LMS menu.

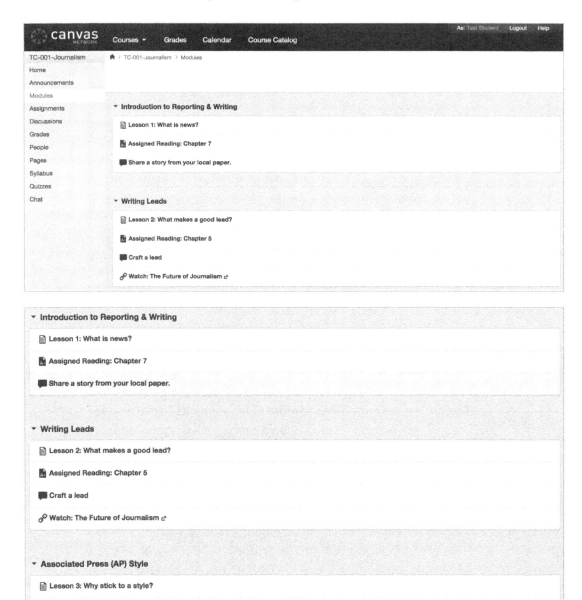

Figure 1.1 *Above*: course content within an LMS; *below*: LMS menus screened out

In the second screenshot, we have shown only that part of the course created by the teacher. This is what we address in this book. Should we need to refer to the use of LMS tools or menus, we will try to generalize rather than mention a specific LMS.

WEB Visit the book's website, where you can view a movie walking you through an LMS. This should help you become familiar with LMS menus and navigation.

1.4 Features of a Learning Management System

Tables 1.1 and 1.2 list the asynchronous and synchronous features of an LMS that you might choose to use in teaching your online course. Refer to Chapter 2 for a walk-through of the basic asynchronous features of an online course. The example we use is from Kristen's Data Visualization course.

1.5 Time: On-Site vs. Online

One of the first challenges for teachers new to the online environment is to understand how time works when teaching online.

When teaching on-site in a classroom, we think in terms of very specific and clearly defined periods of time needed for planning, preparation, class sessions, getting to and from class, feedback on assignments, and office hours.

For example, U.S. universities generally define classes in terms of credits. Each credit represents 15 hours of class time. Most courses are three credits (45 classroom hours). Whether the class is 6, 8, or 15 weeks long, a standard three-credit class will usually have 45 hours of classroom time. In addition, it is expected that a learner will do an additional two to three hours of outside work per classroom hour. So, for a learner:

three-credit class = 45 classroom hours + at least 90 hours outside of class

three-credit class = at least 135 hours in total

The hours per week vary depending upon the length (in weeks) of the course.

But what happens to this time frame when you teach a three-credit asynchronous online class?

Table 1.1 Sample learning management system features list—asynchronous

Feature	Definition
Syllabus	An overview of the course in outline form. It includes objectives, requirements, etc.
Calendar	Schedule of deadlines and course events.
Teacher Announcements	Teacher updates and reminders. They usually appear upon entering the LMS.
Course Email	Correspondence between course members.
Lessons	Content sections usually organized by topic.
Discussion Forums	Ongoing online discussions. They may include text, audio, video, and images.
Wiki	An online environment that can be shared and edited by all members of a collaborative team.
Blog	An online space where one author creates a posting (e.g. article, critique, some type of narrative) and others comment.
Testing/Quizzing	Assessments that determine how successfully outcomes have been achieved. Ungraded self-assessments help learners adjust the pace of and reflect on their learning.
Assignments	Student deliverables such as activities, exercises, and essays. Students upload their work to the LMS and the instructor can grade, comment, and return the student work (see drop boxes below).
Portfolios	Collections of student work from current and possibly past courses.
Workgroups	Online "spaces" confined to a specific group. Members of the group can contribute, comment, and work together within each space.
Drop Boxes	Online tool where students can drop off and pick up assignments.
Social Networks	Applications in which students communicate with each other by posting comments, documents, images, etc.

Table 1.2 Sample learning management system features list—synchronous

Feature	Definition
Chat	An online exchange of text comments and remarks between two or more participants in real time.
Live Classroom/ Live Meeting	Online class sessions in which the teacher and all members are there at the same time and communicate using voice and video. Systems that support live meetings have capabilities for live polling, screen sharing, and live group breakout rooms, and can be recorded.

As with an on-site course, a three-credit online course can be taught within a variety of time frames: 15 weeks, 9 weeks, 5 weeks, etc. (see Table 1.3). As with an on-site course, a three-credit online course offered over 5 weeks will require more time per week than a 15-week course.

Table 1.3 Learning hours per week by length of class in weeks

Weeks	Hours in Class per Week	Hours outside of Class per Week	Total Hours
15	3	6+	135+
9	5	10+	135+
5	9	18+	135+

What Is a Week Online?

An online course's time frame is defined in terms of weeks, as it is in an on-site course. The teacher plans for how much time learners should be spending on work and participation. It should be equal to the time spent on its on-site equivalent. However, the actual time the learner spends online does not correlate to the amount of time spent sitting in a classroom.

Because students have different approaches to how they do things online, the **actual** time the learner spends online in an asynchronous online class is not taken into consideration. Why not? Well, for example, one learner may spend an hour writing out responses or preparing a slide presentation offline, then cut and paste it in when online. The two to three minutes the student spends online putting up the material does not represent the amount of time they have spent working on the presentation. They may also write their discussion forum responses offline, then cut and paste them in.

Another student may do a great deal of their writing while they are online in the course environment. **While class participation is important, class session time is no longer a factor.**

Online "attendance" is determined by looking at both the quantity and quality of learner participation. Requirements for participation are stated very clearly in the syllabus (see Chapter 9).

Flexibility and Convenience

When teachers begin thinking about transforming their class to online, they often feel uncertain about how to plan for time. One thing is for certain: unless a class is in real time (synchronous) or blended (see page 17), "class time" is flexible for both the teacher and the learner.

Because the course is asynchronous, **you can go online any time day or night, whenever it is convenient for you**. This kind of flexibility appeals to people with other commitments such as work or families.

This flexibility is also helpful if you are working with an international class. Learners and teachers can go online whenever convenient, working within their local time zones across the globe.

Deadlines and guidelines play a crucial structuring role in an otherwise open time frame.

Note: Deadlines in an international class need to be stated in a set time zone (e.g. an assignment may be due on May 15 at noon GMT (Greenwich Mean Time—UK) or EST (Eastern Standard Time—east coast, USA). Many LMSs will convert

tip

Learners will vary in how much time they actually spend online. Make learners aware early on that deadlines will help them structure their time in an online course. Frequently remind them of this through online course announcements that are posted in the LMS and simultaneously emailed to students.

times based on students' own time zones. Otherwise, learners are responsible for calculating what that means in their local time zone.

What's the Catch?

The downside of flexibility and convenience is the absence of the kind of structure that you have when planning for classes scheduled at a set time. Here are two key points that will help with this:

- **In the end, the online course must be equal in content and challenge to the on-site course.** Content and learner work should be equal in both courses.

- **The course content is driven by the identical learning outcomes that drive the on-site course.** Use the learning outcomes as a check.

The online process is outcome- and content-driven. A week's content for a 15-week online course is the same as its on-site equivalent.

☑ Course material is sufficient and directly related to learning outcomes.

☑ Learning outcomes for an online course are identical to those of the on-site version.

How Much Time Does Online Teaching and Learning Take?

Time spent on online teaching and learning is difficult to estimate. Generally speaking, there's agreement that teaching online takes more time only because it front-loads course design at the beginning. Once the course is designed and running, many find it takes less time day to day. Also, some of the extra time is regained since you are not traveling back and forth to class.

A teacher goes online regularly. Depending on his schedule, style, and working preferences, a teacher may go online once a day, or several times a day for shorter periods, or do something in between. Sometimes, he will just be "checking in" to see how things are going. Other times, he will spend an hour or more on online activities: posting announcements, initiating discussions, reading, and/or responding to learners. There may be a day when he goes online once, for only 20 minutes, and then, on another day, he may spend two to three hours online. He might download learner work and check it, make notes, then go online to respond when it's more convenient. LMSs often have a feature that notifies the teacher when there is a new activity that needs a response.

Also, online work can be portable. The teacher might, for example, go through homework checks or read learner posts on a smartphone or on paper while on a bus. Flexibility and portability can also make online teaching feel like less time is spent.

What Is the Teacher Doing with her Time?

You will do many of the things a good teacher does in an on-site course. An online course does not just run without instructor involvement and presence. The teacher adds to the experience continually as needed. She adapts and adds to the knowledge base as variations on topics emerge. She has frequent opportunities to apply knowledge, initiate points of interaction, and informally assess knowledge as needed. The following is a list of ways an online teacher uses her time (assuming she is both designing and teaching the course):

- **Designing the course.** Ideally, much of this is done before the course begins. This is the part of the process that we cover in this guide.

- **Teaching.** In an online course, the teacher needs to develop an online persona/profile. Students should see their teacher as present and responsive. Little things such as frequent messages, short video briefs, and personal notes to students can make a teacher's presence felt.

- **Content enrichment.** The teacher adds to the experience continually as needed. She adapts and adds to the knowledge base as variations on topics emerge. She has frequent opportunities to apply knowledge.

- **Posting new material.** The teacher puts up announcements, new learning material, introduces a new discussion topic, initiates a new kind of activity, etc., as needed.

- **Looking at and responding to learner interactions, participation, and work.** This most typically happens in a discussion forum where learners are responding to new material, the teacher's posts, and other learners' posts. It is also possible that this is happening in other ways and "places" online, such as in wikis, the teacher's blog, learners' blogs, group "spaces," presentation areas, etc.

- **Giving feedback on assignments.** Learner assignments require feedback. The time spent on this should be about the same as it is in an on-site course. Providing feedback on students' performance is one of the online teacher's most valuable activities.

- **Class management.** You will do many of the things a good teacher does in an on-site course. An online course does not just run on its own. The teacher spends time on activities such as setting up places for learners to submit their work and communicate (discussion forum threads, drop box folders, chat rooms, etc.), sending out reminders of assignments that are due, grouping/pairing learners for team projects, maintaining an appropriate tone for class, and introducing new assignments and requirements.

Saving Time

One of the most important factors in saving time comes up during the course-building stage. While the course design and implementation of standards may require more upfront time, they can save time in the end. The very first time you create an online course may be quite time-consuming. Each time that course is taught again, you will only be revising and updating. This will get easier as you gain experience.

Reflection

Massive Open Online Courses (MOOCs)

In 2012, massive open online courses (MOOCs) became popularized as an option for individuals to take free online courses without having to be a matriculated student in an educational institution. Since then, millions of people have enrolled in MOOCs taught by instructors from institutions all over the world. MOOCs are often considered an extension of the open education movement, through which institutions and faculty offer their academic content and learning activities to the broader public for free. By creating more complete learning experiences on platforms designed specifically for MOOCs, students and instructors benefit not only from the content shared, but also from the opportunities for rich collaboration and assessment. Institutions in turn benefit from the access MOOCs provide to a larger, nontraditional audience looking for a wide variety of lifelong learning opportunities.

As an instructor, you may be interested in developing a MOOC to reach this broader audience. You may also want to use MOOCs created by other instructors in a blended environment in your own classroom. Regardless of your goal, you should consider a number of things when creating or using a MOOC.

First, the course design of a MOOC should be tailored to a nontraditional audience, with a wide range of skills, abilities, professional experiences, and language capabilities. To accomplish this, it is important to have very clear and detailed directions for how students will participate in the course and what they may gain in return. It is also important to ensure that the topic and content of the MOOC is current, relevant, and provides the appropriate context aligned to clearly stated learning outcomes.

Second, the specific platform through which the MOOC is offered will affect both your experiences and those of your students. There are a variety of platforms currently available, each with its own business model and pedagogical approaches. As you select your platform, you should think about participating in a course as a student yourself in order to fully understand the learning experience and services provided.

Lastly, you should fully understand your goals, or the goals of the offering institution and instructor, for the MOOC. Is the MOOC intended to be used in a blended setting as a traditional college course? Or is it a sample of professional education courses offered by the institution in an effort to market their for-cost programs? Or perhaps the MOOC is offered in order to conduct learning research? All of these are common goals for MOOCs that will significantly affect the student learning experiences contained within.

—Melissa Loble, Sr. Director, Canvas Network

Our goal in this book is to save you as much time as possible during the course-building stage. We do this by emphasizing:

- planning;
- organization;
- consistency;
- simplicity and clarity of language and instructions;
- easy access to or basic production of images, audio, and video;
- models of a variety of activities and assessments; and
- the use of organizing templates.

 You will see this icon whenever we cover a topic that helps you save time during the course-development process.

1.6 Summary and Standards

In this chapter, we provided an orientation for online teaching and learning. The differences between on-site and online teaching were outlined, as well as the key characteristics of teaching online.

☐ Course material is sufficient and directly related to learning outcomes.

☐ Learning outcomes for an online course are identical to those of the on-site version.

Chapter 2 Elements of an Online Course: A Tour

This chapter is a tour of the major elements in an online course. It covers the basic features available within most learning management systems (LMSs). The names of the tools/features may vary across LMSs. We try to cover the most common alternatives.

While it is certainly possible to teach an online course without an LMS, their use is so widespread that we felt it was necessary to provide a general overview of LMS features.

Figure 2.2 (see page 30) presents the elements you normally need to build your online course. It lists the key features of the LMS. Each feature that you plan to use requires some setup before the course goes live. We've also referenced the chapters that are most appropriate for you to review for each item.

Figure 2.1 shows the course description from the online catalog. The illustrations in this chapter are taken from this course.

2.1 Meet the Teacher

We'll begin by introducing you to the teacher who designed the content we are using in this section.

 Kristen Sosulski is Assistant Professor at NYU Stern School of Business and a coauthor of this book. Kristen teaches an executive online course in **Data Visualization** to mid-career adults. In her course, Kristen uses several forms of online assessment, including weekly exercises, collaborative projects, and activities using wikis and blogs. In addition, Kristen holds regular discussions with her students via the **discussion forum** around current business uses of data visualization for communication, analysis, and exploration of data. Support forums are set up for students to solve their homework problems together.

Throughout the book, Kristen will be speaking in her own voice when discussing her course. Her personal comments will always begin with "KS: . . ." and will be in italics.

Course Title: Data Visualization			
Description:	This course is an introduction to the principles and techniques for data visualization. In this course, students will learn visual representation methods and techniques that increase the understanding of complex data and models. Emphasis is placed on the identification of patterns, trends and differences from data sets across categories, space, and time.		
Instructor:	Kristen Sosulski		
Start Date:	2014-09-22	Course End Date:	2014-12-19
Special Note:	This is an online asynchronous course. There are no onsite class meetings.		

Figure 2.1 Course information from an online course catalog

2.2 Features of a Learning Management System (LMS)

There are many features available in LMSs that allow you to create a rich and dynamic course. However, **LMS features are only as good as the content and pedagogical approaches that are employed**. See Figure 2.2 for a partial view of the LMS toolbar.

KS: *In this course, we will look at how I use*:

- *announcements;*
- *syllabus;*
- *lessons;*
- *discussion forums;*
- *assignments;*
- *grade book;*
- *course email;*
- *blogs;*
- *wikis;*
- *tests and quizzes; and*
- *resources.*

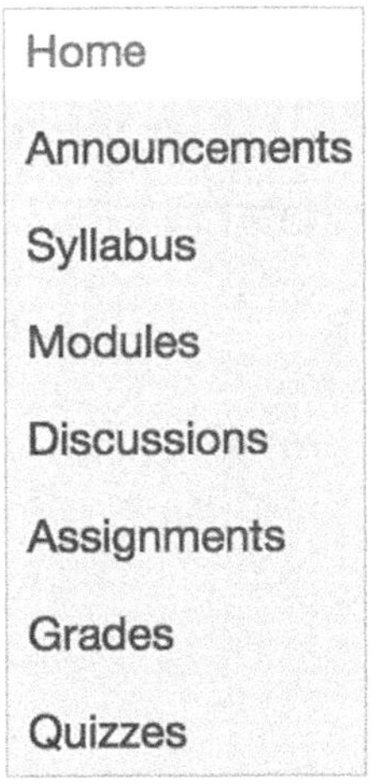

Home

Announcements

Syllabus

Modules

Discussions

Assignments

Grades

Quizzes

Figure 2.2
LMS course toolbar

These features should be standard to any LMS and teachers should plan to use them in their online courses.

Many LMSs are equipped with more advanced features that facilitate student-centered learning and communication. These may include:

- live chat;
- workgroups;
- live Web conferences;
- voting and survey tools; and
- e-portfolios.

We'll introduce you to the basic features and some of the more advanced features of an LMS to orient you to your new teaching space! Let's review these features and explore how they are used.

Announcements

Teacher announcements are usually the first thing students see when entering an online course within an LMS. Announcements can also be emailed to students.

The announcements feature is the place where the teacher communicates important updates to the class.

Welcome to the course!

My name is Kristen Sosulski—I am assistant professor of information systems. If you'd like to read more about me, my bio can be found at: www.stern.nyu.edu/faculty/bio/kristen-sosulski ⬀ .

Review my welcome video before reading on.

This is an asynchronous online course, which means we won't often have an official meeting time or place (actual or virtual). The success of this course depends on you keeping up with the schedule in the course syllabus and your level of involvement with the online activities. Please begin by reviewing the course syllabus. Next, begin thinking about what data visualization means to you. I have discovered that like most interdisciplinary fields data visualization has many definitions and interpretations. I found a few reoccurring themes in the literature that informed the design of this course:

- Data Visualization as Communication focuses on communicating a message through the graphical representation of data.
- Data Visualization as Exploration uses applications, tools, and models that enable and promote the visual exploration of data (big and small). This enables those that work with the data to see patterns, trends, similarities, and differences.
- Data Visualization as Notification uses Information dashboards, mobile apps such as Nike +, and social media analytic tools to evaluate performance as it happens. In a data driven society, information drives decision-making.

Finally, let's get to know one another. If you have not already done so, please post a message in the "Introduce Yourself" forum, describing your background, and what you hope to learn about data visualization. I'm looking forward to hearing from you.

Figure 2.3 An online welcome announcement

KS: *When I post an announcement, it will be waiting for students to read whenever they enter the online course environment. See Figure 2.3 for my "welcome announcement" to students. You'll notice this announcement also contains a short welcome video and introduction to the course. I post a weekly announcement. This reinforces the work I expect students to do over the course of the week.*

 For more examples of course introduction videos, go to the website.

Syllabus

After reading the course announcement, the students review the course syllabus.

Jump to Today

Course Syllabus

Course Title: Data Visualization

Instructor

Professor Kristen Sosulski

Email: ksosulsk@stern.nyu.edu

Office Hours: Available by appointment. Please make an appointment by email.

Course Description

This course is an introduction to the principles and techniques for data visualization. In this course, students will learn visual representation methods and techniques that increase the understanding of complex data and models. Emphasis is placed on the identification of patterns, trends and differences from data sets across categories, space, and time.

Learning Outcomes

- Display data using visual representations that are designed for your target audience, task, and data;
- Experiment with and compare different visualization tools;
- Create multiple versions of digital visualizations using various software packages;
- Identify the appropriate data visualization techniques and tools based on your data;
- Apply appropriate design principles in the creation of presentations and visualizations; and
- Analyze, critique, and revise data visualizations.
- Describe how personal characteristics such as gender, class and ethnicity impact a person's worldview and how the world sees the individual.
- Demonstrate an understanding of global interconnectedness or globalization processes, as seen through subsistence strategies.

Required Text

Tufte, E. R. (2001). The visual display of quantitative information. Graphics Press: Cheshire, CT.

Figure 2.4 An online course syllabus (only a partial syllabus is shown)

The **syllabus** feature is an essential component of the course environment. It **provides structure for the course and outlines course expectations**. When students enter your course for the first time, they should review the syllabus to familiarize themselves with the course requirements. See Figures 2.4 and 2.5 for examples from Kristen's syllabus.

Communication Strategy

There are several ways to contact me:

- Office Hours. I will be available for onsite office hours every Tuesday and Friday from 1pm to 3pm and online by appointment.
- By Phone Appointment. I am available for phone appointments. Please email me to schedule an appointment.
- Email. I am available by email and will respond within 24 to 48 hours. For urgent matters, I would suggest following up by phone at XXX-XXX-XXXX.
- Question and Answer Discussion Forum. Always check the Question and Answer discussion forum to ask a question of the class and see if a response has been posted to your question.

Course Requirements and Grading

Requirement	% of your grade
Weekly exercises	50%
Online class participation	10%
Final team project and online presentation	40%

Figure 2.5 Communication strategies, course requirements, and grading sections of an online course syllabus

Lessons

Online lessons contain the equivalent of the **lectures**, **discussions**, and **activities** that may take place in an on-site classroom.

The lessons are the core instructional containers for your course. You may post a lesson for each unit of instruction. The lessons listing in the syllabus should lead the students through the course's learning outcomes. See Figure 2.6 for a listing of lessons. The students click on the lesson title

---

Lessons

This course includes a series of ten lessons. Most lessons contain videos I've created for purposes of explanation and demonstration. Click on the lesson title to access the materials.

Date	Details	
Sat Aug 29, 2015	Welcome & basic principles of design	due by 11:59pm
Mon Sep 14, 2015	Common tools for creating visualizations	due by 11:59pm
Mon Sep 21, 2015	The process of selecting appropriate displays	due by 11:59pm
Mon Sep 28, 2015	Introduction to using R for visualization	due by 11:59pm
Mon Oct 5, 2015	Advanced use of R for visualization	due by 11:59pm
Mon Oct 12, 2015	Introduction to using python for visualization	due by 11:59pm
Mon Oct 19, 2015	Advanced use of python for visualization	due by 11:59pm
Mon Oct 26, 2015	Introduction to using Tableau for visualization	due by 11:59pm
Mon Nov 2, 2015	Designing effective digital presentations	due by 11:59pm
Mon Nov 9, 2015	Final presentations	due by 11:59pm

Figure 2.6 A listing of the lessons for each week of the online course

Lesson 1: Welcome and basic principles of design

Objective

To understand, identify, and manipulate the chart features that can help and hinder communication to your audience. These include: Chart junk, data-ink ratio, data integrity, data richness, scales, color, and attribution.

Share

Share your experience in data visualization with us by taking this survey.

Watch

Review the following teaching video:

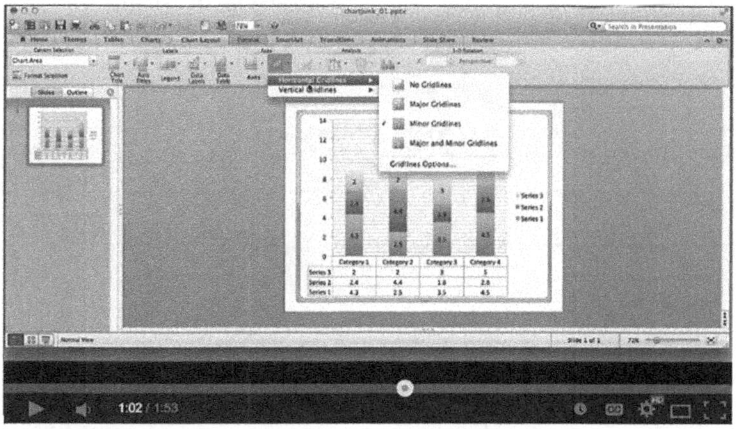

Read

Tufte, E. R. (2001). The visual display of quantitative information. Graphics Press: Chesire, CT.

Sosulski, K. (2012). Design Standards Checklist. Available at: http://bit.ly/designstandards 🖉

Assignment

Complete Assignment 1.

Figure 2.7 The course content sections for a weekly lesson

(e.g. "Welcome & basic principles of design") to see (in this case) the learning objectives, videos, readings, and exercise (see Figures 2.6 and 2.7).

KS: *Notice in the lesson (see Figure 2.7) I've asked students to share their experience in data visualization by completing a survey. This helps activate their prior knowledge and engages their attention right away by getting them to participate. To complete this, they simply click on the survey link and complete the form as shown in Figure 2.8.*

WEB To see the live survey, go to the website.

Also, students are asked to watch a video. This video is an introduction to basic design principles that I have created. In the video, I talk over a series of images that are used to support my explanations.

WEB **For examples of teaching videos, go to the website.**

I've assigned course readings (see Figure 2.7) along with a practice exercise in applying the principles learned in the lesson (see Figure 2.9). I then assess the exercise and provide feedback.

Question 1

Overall, how would you rate your knowledge and skill with the following tools?

R	Average ⬍
Python	Poor ⬍
Adobe Illustrator	Good ⬍
Excel	[Select] ⬍
PowerPoint	[Select] ⬍
Keynote	[Select] ⬍
Google Charts	[Select] ⬍
JavaScript	[Select] ⬍
HTML	[Select] ⬍
CSS	[Select] ⬍
Adobe Dreamweaver	[Select] ⬍

Figure 2.8 Course survey

♠ > Data Visualization > Assignments > Lesson 1 Exercise: World Bank Visualization

Lesson 1 Exercise: World Bank Visualization

Due Thursday by 11:59pm   **Points** 10   **Submitting** a file upload

Data	Download the World Bank (2014) TEU shipping port volume dataset from here: http://bit.ly/portteuvolume ↗
Tools	Excel, PowerPoint, Google Sheets, or Keynote; Google Charts and ManyEyes
Task	Create 3 visualizations of the largest shipping ports using 1. Excel, PowerPoint, Google sheets, or Keynote; 2. Google's Visualization API 3. ManyEyes
Submission	Add your visualizations as images to a document and submit here.

File Upload

Upload a file, or choose a file you've already uploaded.

File: [Choose File] No file chosen

    ⊕ Add Another File

| Comments... |

[Cancel] [Submit Assignment]

Figure 2.9 The weekly assignment referenced in the lesson in Figure 2.7

Discussion Forums

Students go to the discussion forums to participate in the online class discussion. Students can be directed to the forums from a lesson, an assignment, or an announcement from the instructor.

A discussion forum is an asynchronous communication tool that allows class members to exchange ideas in a message board format. Participants post messages or reply to messages posted by other participants.

Communication between participants begins when someone, usually the moderator, posts a topic or question for discussion. Participants begin to communicate with one another by responding to the original post or to the posts of other participants. Discussion forums are used to promote conversations between students and the teacher.

KS: *Figure 2.10 is an example of a discussion forum topic posted by a student in my class who needed help on a topic.*

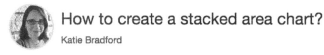

How to create a stacked area chart?
Katie Bradford

Oct 14 at 3:35pm

Hi Everyone! I'm working on a project for my job. Has anyone tried creating a stacked area chart? What's the best tool to do this?

Thanks so much!

-Katie

Figure 2.10 An online class discussion topic posted by a student in the discussion

Assignments

To submit assignments, the teacher may require the students to upload or share their work through the assignments feature of the LMS. Freestanding alternatives for sharing and uploading files include Dropbox, Google Drive, and Office 365.

The assignments feature lets you create assignments that allow students to upload or share documents, presentations, links to websites, and more with the teacher. Each assignment will usually originate in the assignments section of your course, but you can help students navigate to each assignment by including links in each lesson.

KS: *Figure 2.11 is an example of a list of assignments that I set up for students to upload their exercises for each lesson.*

▾ Upcoming Assignments		
📄 The process of selecting appropriate displays	Due Oct 19 at 11:59pm	-/20 pts
📄 Introduction to using R for visualization	Due Oct 31 at 11:59pm	-/20 pts
📄 Final presentations	Due Nov 10 at 11:59pm	-/100 pts
▾ Past Assignments		
📄 Common tools for creating visualizations	Due Sep 14 at 11:59pm	20/20 pts
📄 Welcome & basic principles of design	Due Aug 29 at 11:59pm	20/20 pts

Figure 2.11 Assignments set up by the teacher to collect problem-set assignments from students

Grade Book

The teacher uses the online grade book to communicate grades and feedback to learners.

The **grade book** feature is a tool that displays students' participation, assignment, and project grades. This feature **enables the teacher and the students to review and track academic progress throughout the semester**.

KS: *See Figure 2.12 to see my online grade book. Notice how the exercise titles correspond to those in the assignment section in Figure 2.11. The exercises are underlined to indicate that they link to the assignment details. A grade will appear next to each exercise after it is submitted and graded. In the example, graded items are categorized as either exercises or participation.*

Course Email

The teacher may use the course email feature to send out important messages to students. Mail can be sent to individual students or the entire class. This can be done with the course email feature or the course announcements tool.

Note: Not all LMSs have announcements that automatically notify students with a message via email. In this case, use email to notify students since students probably check their

Grades For Clyde McIntire

🖶 Print grades

	Name	Due	Score	Out of
Participation	**Welcome and basic design principles**	Aug. 29 by 11:59pm	20	20
	Common tools for creating visualizations	Sept. 14 by 11:59pm	20	20
	The process of selecting appropriate displays	Oct. 19 by 11:59pm	-	20
	Introduction to using R for visualization	Oct. 31 by 11:59pm	-	20
	Final presentations	Nov. 10 by 11:59pm	-	20
Weekly Exercises			100%	75% of the final
Quizzes			100%	75% of the final
Total			100%	

Figure 2.12 The online grade book in an LMS

email more frequently than they visit the course announcements.

The course email feature is an asynchronous communication tool that enables the teacher to send messages to class members and also view received, archived, or sent course-related messages. Course email uses the same features as other email systems in that it allows teachers and students to send messages to single or multiple users, which are then stored in their mailbox until deleted.

KS: *See Figure 2.13 for an example of my course's email feature, which archives all of my sent messages to the student groups regarding their final project feedback.*

Resources

In an online course, digital course readings and references are organized in a section commonly referred to as "resources." These resources are cross-referenced in the lessons.

note

Course materials that appear in the resources section of the LMS are cross-referenced in the lessons and assignments sections of the LMS. The resources section provides a place to organize and store files and documents that are then released to students through lessons.

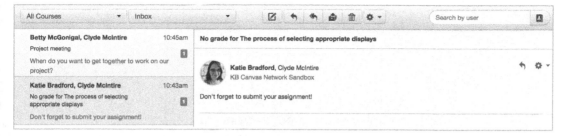

Figure 2.13 The course email feature of an LMS

The **resources feature stores all types of digital and online materials that students are required to review in a repository**, including readings, websites, games, images, sound recordings, and video. To enable easy access to these resources, **the teacher will contextualize the resources within each lesson as appropriate**.

KS: *I use the resources section to post answers to exercises and multimedia resources (see Figure 2.14).*

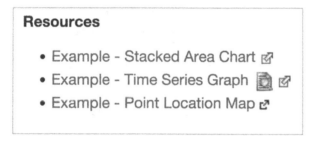

Figure 2.14 The resources section of an LMS

Blogs

Blogs are online journals that enable the teacher and the students to post commentary on course questions, topics, and projects. A single writer serves as the administrator of a blog and is usually the only editor of its content.

Students set up and edit their blogs for the course, and post comments on other blogs attached to the course. Entries are displayed in reverse chronological order (with the most recent being listed first) and include a time and date stamp, which enables readers to see when a new comment has been posted. Blogs offer teachers and students the ability to add commentary to the general course discussion and assignments.

Blogs are usually available in your LMS, but it is more authentic for students to set up their own blog using free online-hosted solutions such as WordPress, Tumblr, or Blogger. The down side is that there is no assurance regarding protecting student privacy since the technology is not controlled or maintained by your institutions. Check with your institutions before implementing free off-the-shelf products.

KS: *In many of my courses, I ask students to create a blog on a subject they find interesting, such as food, new technologies, fashion, etc. The purpose of this assignment is for students to understand both technically and socially how a blog works and how to build the readership of their blog. In real life, blogs are successful based on readership, similar to newspapers and magazines. I ask students to journal about a topic on a weekly basis throughout the course. In many cases, students continue to journal on their topic well after the course is over.*

Using real blogs can take a class activity beyond the scope of a course.

KS: *Figure 2.15 is an example of one of my blog postings where I offer my critique of a data visualization and invite other students to add their critiques as well. In this example, students can observe how I look at data visualizations from a critical standpoint. Typically, I only require each student to read one other student's blog. I do this by pairing students up at the beginning of the course. It can be overwhelming for both the teacher and learners to keep track of every blog posting in the course, as well as the corresponding student comments.*

WEB **See the website for examples of blogs and explanations of how they are used.**

BLOG

November 2, 2014: Wireless Hotspots in London

Take a look at this <u>visualization of wireless hotspots in London</u>.

As we discussed in week 4, this is an example of a geospatial display. The encodings used to represent the hotspot areas are purple transparent bubbles. This type of encoding makes it difficult to see the precise location of the hotspot and the boundaries for the location. Also, notice that all of the bubbles are the same size. What do you think the size of the bubble represents, if anything? Is the color and size used as a marker? Why would the designer use a dual encoding? What else could be improved in this geospatial display?

....

Comment: by Arnold Wilson on 2014-11-03

This map hides the locations of the hotspots, rather than highlighting the hotspots. Without knowledge of the geography of London, it would be impossible to identify a wireless hot spot location.

Figure 2.15 A teacher-led blog

Wikis

The **wiki feature is a shared space in which the teacher and the students are able to post and edit content in order to create a collaborative information resource**. A wiki works upon the premise that users will add, edit, and structure content.

A wiki does not require that users employ a fixed structure for edits and format. Instead, through collaboration, users generate guidelines to structure the content, which may change as the wiki is developed.

KS: *See Figure 2.16 for an example of an activity that I devised using the course wiki. In this exercise, students collectively build a list of design principles that should be used as guidelines to inform the design of any data visualization.*

 See the website for examples of wikis and explanations of how they are used.

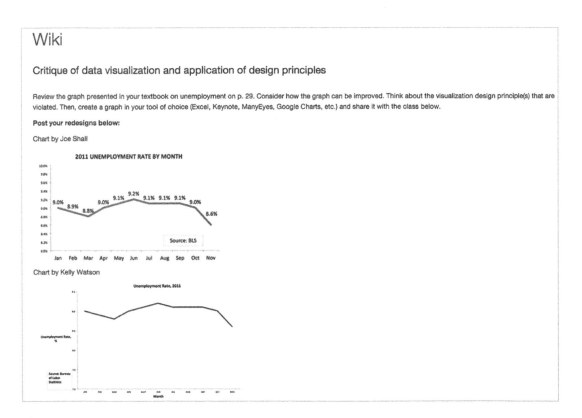

Figure 2.16 A course assignment using a wiki

Tests and Quizzes

Many LMSs are equipped with assessment tools for creating online tests and quizzes. Typically, these tests provide automated feedback to the learners.

KS: *Figure 2.17 is a question from a short self-assessment quiz from my course. I use self-assessment quizzes to enable my students to easily identify gaps in their knowledge and know where they need to improve.*

See Chapter 6 for additional examples.

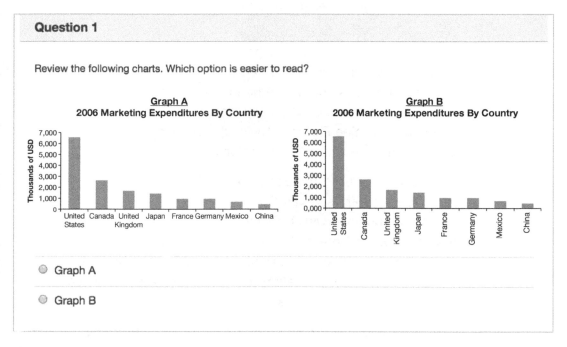

Figure 2.17 An online self-assessment quiz

Live Online Meetings

Many online courses have incorporated the use of live online meetings for office hours, group project meetings with the teacher and group, student group meetings, student presentations to the class, and special guest live lectures and discussions. In Kristen's course, she uses live online meetings to check in with students. She invites students to periodically

Optional Online synchronous meetings

To assist in your learning of data visualization online, there are 3 optional scheduled online working sessions. These sessions are designed around your needs and questions. You are not required to attend. If you wish to attend, please sign up below. In advance of the online meeting, you will receive an email from GoToMeeting with information on how to attend.

Tuesday: 10/7: 8-9am EST: Sign up here.

Tuesday: 10/14: 3-4pm EST: Sign up here.

Wednesday: 10/15: 5-6pm EST: Sign up here.

Figure 2.18 The syllabus section that describes the optional online real-time meetings

join the optional online meetings during key points in the course. This helps her get to know students better, and address questions and concerns in a live setting where the student and teacher can verbally discuss the issues, questions, and concerns. See Figure 2.18 for the section of Kristen's syllabus that describes these optional meetings to students.

The technology used to support live online meetings can range from free software such as Google Hangouts to Skype. Many LMSs are equipped with their own live online meeting tools. It's important to note that many of the free tools limit the number of users that can be online at the same time. The features of online live meeting tools include voice and video capabilities, in addition to screen and document sharing.

 Go to the website for a demonstration of a live online meeting.

2.3 Summary

The features introduced in this chapter are only a sampling of the tools found within many LMSs. While you are becoming acquainted with your institution's system, you should also review the documentation available. Refer to Table 2.1 for an easy-to-use checklist of the main features of the LMS that the teacher can use to create and set up an online course.

Table 2.1 LMS features that are commonly used for an online course

Announcements	Announcements welcome students to the course in a conversational tone, briefly describe the course, direct students to read the syllabus, describe the course format and how the course is organized in the LMS, and direct students to the "Introduce Yourself" forum. Announcements can also update the class on new information or changes to the course.	2, 10, Appendix B
Discussion Forums	In discussion forums, topics are created for online discussions. These should be organized by lesson or around specific activities.	2, 5, 7, Appendix B
Syllabus	Container for: • basic course information; • communication strategy; • course time frame and format; • assignments; • activity grade percentages; • criteria for class participation; • technical requirements and support; and • course outline.	1, 3, 5, 7, 9, Appendix B
Lessons	A lesson should be created for each week or two of the course. The lesson should at least include the following: • lesson title; • start and end dates; • introduction with learning outcomes; • video/audio mini-lecture; • required and recommended readings; • activities; • assessments to measure learning in the lesson, such as assignments (include due dates and times); • self-assessments or practice exercises; and • summary.	5, 6, 8, 9, 10, Appendix B
Resources	A place to organize and store files. These can be linked and/or uploaded to the resources section of the site and cross-referenced in lessons, assignments, forums, etc.	6, 8, 10

Table 2.1 *Continued*

Drop Boxes/ Assignment Submission Area	Drop-off place for assignments that require students to submit papers or projects. Create a drop box for each assignment then link to a lesson for students to easily submit their work in context.	7, 10
Blogs, Wikis, and Workgroups	Tools for setting up collaborative activities.	3, 5, 7, 10
Live Online Meetings, Audio/Video and Screen Sharing	Tools for setting up activities that require verbal synchronous (real-time) communication, such as group brainstorming meetings, faculty office hours, and small group presentations to the instructor.	1, 2, 7

Chapter 3 Language and Writing Style

Clear, concise writing addresses the needs of all types of online learners. It removes one more barrier to good communication and understanding. This chapter reviews the basic pitfalls to avoid and techniques to embrace when writing for your online class. The chapter also includes a section on writing instructions for activities and course announcements.

3.1 Rationales for Clear, Concise Writing

Clear, concise writing always supports good communication and learning.

Using clear, concise writing models an accessible style that learners might emulate. Whatever the subject, teachers may also find that commenting on learners' writing advances the learning process. The tone used in such exchanges should be supportive.

3.2 Writing Style

Less is more.

—Motto of Ludwig Mies van der Rohe

The following advice on writing style has been around for a while but is still relevant today:

A sentence should contain no unnecessary words, a paragraph no unnecessary sentences . . . This requires not that the writer make all his sentences short, or that he avoid all detail and treat his subject only in outline, but that every word tell.

(Strunk, 1918)

In other words, keep it simple! This is not always as easy as it sounds. Sometimes, the only way to get there is to take some time to edit carefully until it just becomes natural to write clearly and concisely.

☑ **The writing style is clear, concise, and direct.**

3.3 Paragraphs

> Enormous blocks of print look formidable to a reader. He has a certain reluctance to tackle them; he can lose his way in them. Therefore breaking a paragraph in two, even though it is not necessary to do so for sense, meaning, or logical development, is often a visual help.
>
> (Strunk, 1918)

This is especially true online. We will revisit the topic of short paragraphs again in Chapter 8.

3.4 Sentences

Sentences should be concise and clear. Let's look at some examples for simplifying, inspired by Strunk and White (1979):

Tom is the type of person who **likes to eat out with a group** of friends.

Tom likes to eat out with friends.

The reason why **I don't go out alone at night** is that **I'm afraid to do so**.

I'm afraid to go out alone at night.

And here are some examples from rewrites from this guide:

Once the class begins, the teacher's role is to **focus on learner participation and assessment**.

Once the class begins, the teacher focuses on learner participation and assessment.

There are **some learners** that may **fall into more than one** of these **categories**.

Some learners fall into more than one category.

 Sentences and paragraphs are brief and to the point.

3.5 Words and Phrases

Below is the classic set of instructions on the use of words in writing:

> [One] can often be in doubt about the effect of a word or a phrase, and one needs rules that one can rely on when instinct fails. I think the following rules will cover most cases:
>
> i. Never use a metaphor, simile or other figure of speech which you are used to seeing in print.
>
> ii. Never use a long word where a short one will do.
>
> iii. If it is possible to cut a word out, always cut it out.
>
> iv. Never use the passive where you can use the active.
>
> v. Never use a foreign phrase, a scientific word or a jargon word if you can think of an everyday English equivalent . . .
>
> (Orwell, 1946)

Avoid Jargon

Jargon, unlike technical terms, can be replaced by standard English words and phrases. Obviously, avoiding jargon makes your content understandable to more people.

Using jargon may mean that a learner who is not familiar with a term will either guess at the meaning, just ignore it, or stop what they are doing to look it up. The former two options may lead to misunderstanding. The latter option breaks the flow of concentration on the topic.

Avoid Colloquialisms

While it is possible that your students will be from the same dialect group, all speaking the same first language, it is unlikely. Your language and tone can be informal without being casual. Again, by avoiding colloquialisms, you widen the circle of learners who will understand. The class will also feel more inclusive.

Avoid Clichés and Tired Phrases

Well-worn phrases or clichés lose their meaning with so much use. Try making the point in your own words or by using your own devices. Another reason to avoid tired phrases is that they may seem alien and even nonsensical in other parts of the world where people have learned another dialect or form of English. Even native English speakers, living in the country where these phrases originated, may be confused by clichés or well-worn similes or metaphors. Some examples of confusing or worn phrases: a *friend in need is a friend indeed*, *better late than never*, *a stitch in time saves nine*, etc.

☑ Familiar or common words are used when possible.

☑ Jargon, clichés, and colloquial and idiomatic expressions are avoided.

Explain Acronyms

Acronyms are tricky. It's simply not efficient to write out the full names of every organization, field, etc. Give the full name along with the acronym the first time it is mentioned. However, you cannot assume that the learner will recognize the acronym the next time she sees it. The full name should always be within reach either in an easily accessible glossary or somewhere close by within the learning segment.

e.g. MOOC = massive open online course

Provide a Glossary or Definitions if Needed

However much you succeed at simplifying your language, learners may still need a glossary. Access to the definition of a word, term, or acronym should be immediate.

The most immediate access possible is to click on the word and see the definition appear. This could happen, for example, by creating a link to its definition. If this is not possible, the definition might just be included somewhere on the same page, perhaps in a text box.

A glossary that requires the learner to leave what he is reading to get to a definition that is two or more clicks away is pedagogically unsound.

If the above suggestions are not possible, consider giving the students the special terms in the introduction of the lesson, as Scott Thornbury does (see page 184). This allows the students to look them up before they begin the lesson.

☑ **The meaning of special terms, abbreviations, and acronyms is easy to access.**

3.6 Tone

> When developing presentations ensure that your tone is conversational. People learn better when the words of a multimedia presentation are in conversational style rather than formal style.
>
> (Mayer, 2005, p. 6)

Ideally, learners feel comfortable and motivated when they are in the online environment. Using an informal or conversational tone and encouraging students to do the same helps to create a safe environment online.

Difficult discussions, whether teacher-to-learner or learner-to-learner, should be saved for email correspondence. Openly encourage learners to keep conflicts or personal disagreements out of the classroom space.

An announcement on online etiquette, including guidelines on tone and attitude, is best given to learners before the class begins in an orientation or at the beginning of class. This should include suggestions on:

- tone (see above);
- using clear, correct language;
- avoiding "flaming" (angry/screaming/using all caps);
- avoiding sarcasm; and
- being tolerant.

☑ **A supportive second-person conversational tone is used throughout the course.**

3.7 Writing Instructions and Announcements

> The areas where clarity is most crucial are labeling and instructions—the elements that guide users through the functions of a page. Navigation is not a place for unclear language—link labels must be self-explanatory to guide users to their destination. Clarity in form labels is important, too. Ambiguous form labels lead to incorrect data. In general, all instructions should use clear and concise language.
>
> (Horton, 2006)

In an online course, the primary method for communicating with learners about expectations is through writing. Many of the things you will be writing are assignment and activity instructions, and course announcements.

The **instructions for activities and assignments must be clear and simply stated**. If items are sequenced, use numbers. If they are a list of options, use bullet points. Anticipate the questions that students may ask, and try to include them in the activity and assignment instructions. Instructions for assignments should generally include:

- due date and time;

- submission location in the LMS; and

- grading criteria.

Refer to Figure 3.1 for an example.

Course announcements serve as **organizers** for students to understand what they need to do for a given week (see Figure 3.2). Be clear and point students to the areas in the LMS where they can find the information they need. Avoid using course announcements as a way to deliver or introduce new material; the modules/lessons area of the LMS is designed to present the week-by-week details and content. **Announcements should be sent out to the class weekly.**

 Instructions and requirements are stated simply, clearly, and logically.

Final papers

Due Oct 5, 2015 by 5pm   **Points** 100

Final Paper Instructions

Write a 5-page book review of Clay Shirky's *Here Comes Everybody*.

In your review address the following questions:

- Why are tools not enough to foster collaboration?
- A group's complexity grows faster than its size. Explain.
- Define user-generated content.
- Describe and provide examples of the three types of social loss described by Shirky.
- Why are tools such as MeetUp successful?
- Discuss the important that Shirky places on failure.

Requirements

Upload your paper by 10/5/2015 by 5:00 p.m. EST. The paper must be submitted as a Microsoft World (.doc) file. Please name your file lastname_firstname.doc.

The paper must be written in 12 point Arial or Times New Roman font. Double-spaced with one-inch margins. A title page is required and **does not** count toward the total page count. APA style must be followed and all quoted or referenced material from the book must be cited appropriately.

Figure 3.1 Instructions for a final paper assignment

Welcome to Week 5!

Kristen Sosulski

Oct 16 at 11:38am

Dear Class,

Welcome to week 5 of Collaboration Technologies. For this week please continue reading *Here Comes Everybody*. The details are explained in the week 5 lesson.

Later this week I will be posting the final paper assignment. I will make an announcement in the course and send an email notification indicating where you can find the assignment description details.

Please feel free to contact me with any questions! Happy reading!

Best,

Professor Sosulski

Figure 3.2 Course announcement message

3.8 Labeling

It is critically important that labeling on graphs, charts, diagrams, and images is in a typeface that is clear and large enough to read. The label itself should stand out from the background enough to be seen. We have tried to do this in this book, for example.

 Labeling in all presentation materials is accurate, readable, and clear.

Labeling throughout the course should be well written and accurate. If an image or chart is labeled, the words should be placed so that they stand out and are clear. Links should be descriptive so that students understand what they link to (e.g. Click here to post your response on discussion forum).

3.9 Language in Audio, Video, and Multimedia

Spoken language is fleeting. You can't go back to review something you've heard as easily as you can when reading. Even in the digital age, reviewing audio material if you've missed a word or phrase is awkward and time-consuming. Needing to do so repeatedly is frustrating.

When creating audio for presentations, it is critical that you follow the guidelines on language laid out in this chapter. Keep it as simple as you can.

Pacing

Spoken language has a temporal dimension. The reader controls his pace when reading. Most often, the listener has no control over the pace of spoken language. Even native speakers may have difficulty following directions that race along too quickly.

In the global world of online education, there will be many nonnative speakers of English listening to the spoken language in online courses and presentations. **The pace of speaking is critically important**. It is important to pause at key moments between discrete elements. This is similar to paragraph breaks in written language. We advise using short sentences and paragraphs in written language. The same is true when speaking.

On the other hand, it is important to keep your speaking natural. It is not necessary to speak slowly. Just don't speak too quickly. A well-done documentary or news feature should give you a good model to follow.

Don't script your spoken sections if you are not used to doing so. Scripted material can sound artificial. Just listen to some good examples of spoken text then listen to yourself. Spending some time on this will get you to the point where you are in control of the pacing.

Quality of Sound

 The sound quality of audio and video is good enough to be clearly understood.

 The pacing of spoken language is natural sounding yet slow enough to be understood by a variety of learners.

tip

Check to see if your school/institution has a media center that lends out high-quality webcams or microphones if you don't have one of your own.

3.10 Accuracy

It's good practice to give everything you've written a double check for accuracy. It should be relatively error-free.

 The course material has been edited for language and grammar.

3.11 Summary and Standards

Keep it simple, clear, and concise.

- [ ] The writing style is clear, concise, and direct.
- [ ] Sentences and paragraphs are brief and to the point.
- [ ] Familiar or common words are used when possible.
- [ ] Jargon, clichés, and colloquial and idiomatic expressions are avoided.
- [ ] The meaning of special terms, abbreviations, and acronyms is easy to access.
- [ ] Labeling in all presentation materials is accurate, readable, and clear.
- [ ] Instructions and requirements are stated simply, clearly, and logically.
- [ ] The course material has been edited for language and grammar.
- [ ] A supportive second-person conversational tone is used throughout the course.
- [ ] The pacing of spoken language is natural sounding yet slow enough to be understood by a variety of learners.
- [ ] The sound quality of audio and video is good enough to be clearly understood.

Chapter 4 Visual Design Basics

Online material should be attractive. This is different than simply clear text and well organized material. It should be graphically appealing.

(Madden, 1999)

4.1 Rationales for Good Visual Design

Good design is a lot like clear thinking made visual.
—Motto of Edward Tufte

Good visual design supports understanding through simplicity, clarity, and organization. Nothing in the design of the page distracts from communication. An open, clear, attractive page design enhances communication.

We learn from Howard Gardner (1993) (see page 81) that we do not all process visual information in the same way. Simply because a medium is visual does not mean that it will automatically appeal to the visual learner. In fact, the visual learner may be turned off by dense, confusing visual design. This in turn may interfere with comprehension, concentration, and learning.

4.2 Visual Design Online

Classroom teachers in some fields depend on using visuals in the classroom (e.g. art, sciences, etc.). When working online, we must keep in mind that content presented in text is visual as well. This text is different than the text in a book because, online, text replaces speaking.

Let's also keep in mind that our "digital pros" (see page 14) are used to visual variety. We live in an age when content is

Personal Perspective

Marjorie Vai

I, as a strongly visual learner, have been completely shut down at times when facing dense text. It's as if I'm looking at a block of some kind of intricate design. When, for some reason, I am obliged to stick to my reading, I can do it but become frustrated by the lack of attention to readability.

You should be aware of this when creating online content. For the visual learner, great blocks of unbroken text online are the equivalent of listening to an on-site teacher reading from a book in a drone—without intonation, stress, rhythm, pauses, illustrations, or nonverbal language.

The same is true when colors are overused. I need to extract understanding and meaning through a great deal of visual noise. This would be like listening to a lecture in a room with a very noisy factory next door.

While all educators would probably agree with these two listening examples, some are unaware of the effects of the text examples mentioned above on the visual learner.

A highly respected colleague once insisted that a good teacher is a good teacher, whether on-site or online. Well, this is not exactly true. A teacher who is very good in the classroom needs to transform her skills to a different form of delivery. If she is clear and articulate on-site, she transfers that skill by paying attention to her writing, making text easily readable, and using an open layout online. If she is well organized in her oral presentations, she will want to pay attention to visual layout and organizing cues, such as numbering, bullets, headings, and subheadings, when presenting online. There is a difference. But it is an easy adjustment once you are aware of it.

reduced, broken up, and illustrated. Things move fast. We can discuss the pros and cons of this, but we can't disagree that it has changed the way many think, especially the young. This includes communication style, modes of collaboration, and ways in which they find and use information.

As with language, the laws that govern good graphic design have been around for a long time. However, they need to be adjusted for the online medium.

There are ways to add stress, rhythm, emphasis, pauses, and room to think in the presentation of online text and page layout. In this chapter, we cover text, layout, and graphic elements that enhance the learning experience.

Personal Perspective

Kristen Sosulski

My suggestion: **read this chapter, then read it again.**

In my work, I've noticed that a common oversight of online teachers is their lack of attention to visual and aesthetic design. There are a lot of textual materials in an online course. It's easy to overlook the format of those materials.

The ways that learners interact with the online course is directly related to how well it is organized and designed. **Dense text and unrelated images can overload and overwhelm the learner.** This can impede learning.

4.3 Page Layout

Once you know how to design and manipulate the space outside, inside, and around your content, you'll be able to give your readers a head start . . . and perhaps even begin to see your own content in a new light.

(Boulton, 2007)

Above all else, an online layout must be open. Open means that there is enough white space on the page to keep the mind clear, enough white space to allow the online student to feel that he is not overburdened by the task at hand.

 Page layout is uncluttered and open, and includes a significant amount of white space.

Spaces Surrounding Text

less is more

> The opportunity lost by increasing the amount of blank space is gained back with enhanced attention on what remains . . . When there is less we appreciate everything much more.
>
> (Maeda, 2006, p. 56)

The space between lines and paragraphs provides white space. It enhances the readability of the text. And the space between paragraphs should be noticeably deeper than the space between lines.

Again, when text is tight and unbroken, the first thing a person sees is a dark gray shape. He must then try to move past that to seek out the words and begin reading. As we noted on page 000, short paragraphs improve readability.

There should also be space to the left and right of the text. This is also important when using text boxes. When text abuts the sides of a text box, it is difficult to read. Space should be added surrounding the text.

☑ There is sufficient space between lines, paragraphs, and to the right and left of text so that it stands out and is easy to read.

Keep Line Length Short

> Research shows that reading slows as line lengths begin to exceed the ideal width, because the reader then needs to use the muscles of the eye or neck to track from the end of one line to the beginning of the next line. If the eye must traverse great distances on a page, the reader must hunt for the beginning of the next line.
>
> (Lynch & Horton, 2009, pp. 192–193)

Because the size of browser screens can be varied at will, line length can vary. **When lines of text are too long, they are difficult to read.** In an environment where learning is an outcome of good readability, restricting line length is critical.

However, restricting the length of lines may not be within your control. You may be working within an LMS that has already predetermined the line length of your content. At times, the best you can do is to recommend that the students keep their browser window narrower for comfortable line length.

Justify Text

When text is justified (i.e. evenly lined up with the edge of the paper) on both sides, it can look neater than text that is only justified on the left. However, it is not as readable as left-justified text for two reasons: the spaces between words vary, and/or words are broken at the end of lines with hyphens. Without specifically adjusting the text, line by line, some strange things can happen. You may, at times, notice "rivers" of space flowing down between words. This is distracting. Generally speaking, the ability to vary line lengths is considered a benefit. **Always use left-justified text with ragged right margins as we have in this guide.**

 Text is left-justified and right margins are ragged.

Headings and Subheadings

> On the web, more than any other prose medium, the look of text layout strongly affects how readers relate to written content. The contrast produced by headlines, subheads, lists, and illustrations give users visual "entry points," drawing their eyes down the page and into the content.
>
> (Lynch & Horton, 2009, p. 236)

UNITS, Lessons, Sections, Segments, . . .

Headings and subheadings signal the organization of the content. Each of the examples above has a specific size, typeface, and/or thickness assigned to it. Headings are generally left-justified like the text. **Headings and subheadings organize the content and should be used consistently.**

 Headings and subheadings are used consistently to logically organize content.

4.4 Text

When information is presented in its most basic form, it's easy to draw attention to aspects that are important. For example, in a block of text, emphasizing a word or phrase is a matter of

---

Leading
[noun]
The amount of space between lines of text.

---

changing one attribute: color, typeface, or style. In a simple layout, drawing the eye to an important section can be accomplished by changing one attribute: background color, leading, or typeface. If, however, the page already contains elements of emphasis, highlighting what is important becomes difficult since so many elements are already competing for attention. And if more and more emphasis is added in an effort to make each element stand out, the resulting design is chaotic and confusing.

(Horton, 2006)

Typefaces

Figure 4.1 is a list of **Web-safe typefaces**. That is, these are typefaces that one can count on being accessible on almost all computers. Most likely, these are the typefaces that you will be using in an LMS.

It is important to keep in mind that typefaces online have a much lower resolution (measured in dots per inch) than typefaces on paper. Therefore, the general rule is to keep it simple, as always!

The first two typefaces listed in Figure 4.1, Georgia and Times New Roman, are **serif** typefaces. This means that there is more detail in the form of serifs. Serifs are small, tail-like extensions that you find on some of the letters. Also, the thickness of the lines may vary in a serif typeface. It has been argued that serif typefaces are more readable on paper because the detail may help to define the letters.

Other typefaces listed in Figure 4.1, such as Arial and Helvetica, are **sans serif** (without serif) typefaces. These are simpler in form. They tend to be more readable online because of the lower resolution. Small details such as serifs may reduce readability. You can see the clear difference between serif and sans serif type at the bottom of Figure 4.1.

Georgia
Times New Roman
Arial
Helvetica
Tahoma
Trebuchet MS
Verdana
Andale Mono
Courier New
Comic Sans
Impact
serif
sans serif

Figure 4.1
A list of Web-safe typefaces

Type Size

Type size is another important factor in online readability. Again, because resolution on a computer screen is much lower than on paper, larger type is easier to read because you have more dots available per inch to define the letters. The letters will be crisper and clearer looking. The online platform or LMS you are using will likely set the type size to a standard, but if not, we recommend that you use at least 12-point type for online.

WEB **See the resources on the website for more details on type.**

☑ A universal sans serif Web typeface (e.g. Verdana) assures access across platforms and enhances screen readability.

☑ Type size should be large enough to be easily readable by all students.

Bold and Italic—Use Sparingly

Bold type can be used very effectively for emphasis when used sparingly. See examples throughout this guide.

Italic is generally used for titles of works and for instances when words are used in an unusual way. **Italic type is more difficult to read online because of the resolution.** Use it sparingly also.

☑ Bold and italic typefaces are used sparingly only to emphasize important items.

Underlining—Only for Links

In an online environment, underlining is used only for links.

☑ Underlining is used only for links.

Avoid Using All Caps

All caps should only be used for acronyms. Avoid using them for emphasis. They are not as readable as lower-case letters because they are more uniform in size (e.g. "HIGHLIGHT" vs. "highlight").

☑ Words in all caps are avoided.

Color—Use with Care

Color can make an impact if it is used with care. Save lighter colors for special emphasis such as highlighting. However, keep in mind that **contrast is an important factor in readability**.

Pale yellow works so well for highlighting because it contrasts strongly with black type. If you go darker than that, you begin to sacrifice contrast and, consequently, readability.

The same is true for colored backgrounds. Black against white, or dark blue or black against pale yellow or any other very pale color, will work well. The reverse will work as well (e.g. pale yellow type on a dark blue background). Diminish the contrast and you diminish readability.

Color type is also good for emphasis. A dark color type used for heads can make them pop out.

Keep contrast in mind. Red type may get the learner's attention, but will she be able to read it easily? Keep in mind that learners are looking at a backlit screen in most cases. This is not the same as red print on paper. **Readability depends on contrast.**

There are many ways that color can be used to clarify, enhance, and engage. However, **always keep focused on color's power to distract**. As with all enhancements, it should be used sparingly and with purpose.

Look at Figure 4.2. The colored names across the top row indicate the background color in each column. The color of the type is indicated in the first column. Looking at it in black and white is very helpful because the contrast, or lack of contrast, is so clear. Keep this chart in mind when using colored type and/or colored backgrounds/highlights.

Notice the use of grays on the pages of this guide. Since we did not have access to color, we used gray the way you might use color. Gray/white/black typefaces, used in combination with certain shapes or graphic elements, signal a certain type of activity, comment, or reading.

background colors							
white	yellow	orange	red	violet	blue	green	black
	white	white	white	white	white	white	white
yellow		yellow	yellow	yellow	yellow	yellow	yellow
orange	orange		orange	orange	orange	orange	orange
red	red	red			red	red	red
violet	violet	violet			violet	violet	violet
blue	blue	blue	blue	blue		blue	blue
green	green	green	green	green	green		green
black	black	black	black	black	black	black	black

Figure 4.2 A color chart

WEB You can see an example of this chart in color on the website.

☑ Color is used with purpose.

☑ There is good contrast between text and background.

4.5 Graphic Elements

Symbols and Icons

Symbols and icons can be very useful in signaling small elements in a website that appear over and over again. For example, here are three of the icons we've used in this book to signal key items that recur:

WEB To indicate that there is an example or related material on the website.

🕐 To indicate a time-saving suggestion.

☑ or ☐ To signal a standard.

tip

Free icons can be found online. Often, you can just cut and paste them into the text.

Icons immediately signal the presence of a certain feature. The learner can then scan the material to look for where the particular feature shows up.

You can also use icons to signal certain types of activities. When the student sees the icon, he should know what to expect. Icons are helpful for all learners, but especially visual learners.

 Another way to signal a certain type of activity is through color-coding. You may use a translucent screen of color for emphasis. **Look at Scott Thornbury's course example on the website.** It has a pale gray background color, and an icon and title to indicate a specific kind of activity or reading. This makes the course very easy to follow. As with all graphic elements, they must be used consistently throughout the course.

 Visual elements (e.g. icons, shading, and color) are used consistently to distinguish between different types of course elements (e.g. lessons, assignments, audio, and video).

Bullets and Numbers in a Series

Items in a series stand apart when they are bulleted. When the series of items occurs in a sequential order, as is the case with most instructions, numbers are used in place of bullets. This distinction is very important.

 Use bullets or numbers to set apart items that can be listed.

 Numbers are used to identify sequential steps in a task or process. They are also used for rankings and setting priorities.

 Bullets are used to highlight a series of items that are not prioritized or sequential.

Example

A judicious use of a selection of visual design elements lets the student instantly know where he is, what he is doing, and how things are ordered.

Let's look at an example to illustrate some of the most basic elements. Figure 4.3 is a segment of text that needed to be included in the body of an online teacher-training course. The text looks almost like a solid block. The eye tends to see an all-over pattern first. This does not make it very easy to read, especially on a computer screen.

We did the following to rework the text block in Figure 4.4 (page 70):

- **Increased text size.** In this case, we have only increased it by one point. It is now 11 points. If this were actually online, 12–14 points would be better.
- Changed type to Helvetica, a **sans serif** typeface.
- Added **space between the letters and lines**.
- Created **white space between items that can be naturally broken up**. You will most certainly be able to break up, or chunk, text as we have done below.

bad visual example (handwritten annotation)

As Scharle and Szabó (2000) state, *most language teachers have experienced the frustration of investing endless amounts of energy in their students and getting very little response.* Teachers have had students who don't do their homework, are reluctant to speak in the target language or who don't learn from their mistakes. This often happens because students rely on the teacher as the one who should be in charge of whatever happens in the classroom. The answer to this is autonomy. For this to work, we need to have responsible learners. Scharle and Szabó define them as: *those who accept the idea that their own efforts are crucial to progress in learning, and behave accordingly.* They are also willing to cooperate with the teacher and others in the learning group for everyone's benefit.
What makes an autonomous learner?
– Does things beyond what the teacher asks or requests. For instance, may do extra grammar exercises either in print or on line.
– Goes beyond what the teacher presents in class. For example, looks up a new word in a dictionary even if the teacher didn't "teach" it during the lesson.
– Likes to find ways to stay in contact with the target language outside the classroom. For example, may regularly keep up with English language sites of interest on the internet

Figure 4.3 A text segment for an online course

The difference here is that, in addition to breaking material up, we've added more space by isolating some pieces of information, or just adding more space between paragraphs to add more contrast.

- Used **bullets** to emphasize a list of related items. Notice more space is added in front of the bullets.

good visual example

Learner Autonomy

As Scharle and Szabó (2000) state, *most language teachers have experienced the frustration of investing endless amounts of energy in their students and getting very little response.*

Teachers have had students who don't do their homework, are reluctant to speak in the target language or who don't learn from their mistakes. This often happens because students rely on the teacher as the one who should be in charge of whatever happens in the classroom.

The answer to this is autonomy.

For this to work, we need to have responsible learners. Scharle and Szabó define them as: *those who accept the idea that their own efforts are crucial to progress in learning, and behave accordingly.* They are also willing to cooperate with the teacher and others in the learning group for everyone's benefit.

What makes an autonomous learner?

An autonomous learner:

- **Does things beyond what the teacher asks** or requests. For instance, may do extra grammar exercises either in print or on line.

- **Goes beyond what the teacher presents** in class. For example, looks up a new word in a dictionary even if the teacher didn't "teach" it during the lesson.

- Likes to find ways to **stay in contact with the target language outside the classroom**. For example, may regularly keep up with English language sites of interest on the internet.

Figure 4.4 A reworked example of text from Figure 4.3 for an online course

- Used **bold type for emphasis**. In this case, the use of bold creates a summary of the topic. The basics jump out. As with other elements that are used for emphasis, such as colored text or italics, bold type is only effective if used sparingly. If too much text is in bold, the sense of emphasis is lost.

- Added a **heading**. Colored, bold, or larger type distinguishes the headings from the content, and signals the topic. Headings and subheadings emphasize, distinguish, and organize. It is critical that headings and subheadings are used consistently otherwise they lose their very important organizing function.

Visual Design Basics in the Online Class

How do you bring these ideas of basic visual design into the online class? The truth is, at times, it may be difficult. You can follow most of the standards we've laid out for type, justification, headings, bullets, and numbers fairly easily. Below is an example of a toolbar for a discussion forum. While LMSs may vary, this one is fairly typical.

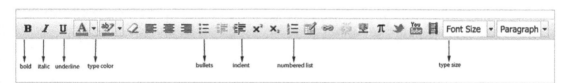

Figure 4.5 A typical editing toolbar in an LMS

tip

If you just begin by making sure that the typeface is readable for everyone, and that there is a good amount of space between lines and blocks of type, and on the page in general, you're making a very good start!

We have labeled the buttons that relate to the items in this chapter (see Figure 4.5).

Depending on how rigid your online environment is, the issue of white space and space between lines, letters, and paragraphs may be challenging. Be mindful of the impact of visual elements.

71

4.6 Visual Design with Audio, Video, and Multimedia

We covered issues of the pacing of audio content in the last chapter. However, when combining audio and visual elements, whether in video or slide presentations, pacing and quality of sound are not the only considerations. When audio is combined with visual communication, one needs to be sure that the visual supports the content rather than confusing it.

Combining Written and Spoken Language

All of the guidelines on visual design apply to slides and video, as well as screen design. If text is inserted in video or presentation slides, it must, of course, be readable and clearly presented. But this alone does not guarantee that what you present will be clearly understood.

You have probably seen presentations with a great deal of text on the screen at the same time as the speaker is talking. He may have summarized what he is saying in lists or paragraphs on the screen. In his mind, the speaker may think that he is reinforcing what he is saying by doing this. In fact, the messages compete with one another for attention. In the end, they confuse.

The best presenters keep words on-screen to an absolute minimum. One cannot read attentively while listening and one cannot listen attentively while reading. Attempting to do so becomes a mental juggling act.

 Look at one of Steve Jobs' presentations on the website. He was renowned for the engagement level and clarity of his presentations.

On the other hand, you may have text that you want the viewers to pay special attention to by reading it themselves. If this is the case, it adds variety to the presentation to have the viewers read it without hearing you read it as well. Of course, you must give them enough time to read it. You can ensure that they have done so by incorporating a brief summary of the content when you continue speaking.

☑ Content is designed simply and clearly to avoid information overload (e.g. avoid narrating while written text is visible, using distracting images for decoration, presenting too much information at once, etc.).

☑ Avoid combining spoken and written narrative in presentations.

Visual Interest

A topic will be more interesting and easier to understand if spoken language is combined with clear, relevant, and helpful visual material. This is especially true in subject areas that rely on or are about visual matter such as art, biology, math, engineering, etc.

Under any circumstances, one is usually advised to avoid "talking head" videos. This is certainly true when presenting long lectures that will most certainly become tedious if they go on for more than 10 minutes. If video of "talking head" lectures is provided, the speaker should break the content up into small

---

John Medina's 10-Minute Lecture

Dr. John Medina is a developmental molecular biologist who has won numerous teaching awards. In his book *Brain Rules*, Medina describes a lecture format that has improved student learning and maintained engagement in his university courses:

- Limit each lecture segment to 10 minutes, no more.
- Present meaning before detail. Give a one-minute gist to introduce each segment.
- Remind learners "where we are" with each segment, and explain how the current segment relates to the rest of the class session.
- "Bait the hook" at the end of each segment in order to buy yourself another 10 minutes. Use emotion and relevance to hook students' interest.

(Stein & Graham, 2014)

segments. We discuss this "chunking" later in the book in more detail.

On the other hand, it is important for the students to get a feel for the teacher as a person. Weaving videos of the teacher with short commentary throughout a course will help students relate to the teacher.

In the end, just try to put yourself in the shoes of the students when creating videos and presentations. Would you be engaged or not in their position?

 Videos should be no longer than 10 minutes in length.

4.7 Visual Design and Mobile Devices

There may be no way to predict how students will access their online course and course materials. However, chances are that most will do so on some kind of mobile device, whether a tablet, electronic reader, laptop, or smartphone. Good visual design and readability are critically important knowing that students will most likely be using smaller screens.

In the best of circumstances, your institution's delivery system for online courses will have an additional interface for tablets and smartphones. If it does not, there are ways to adapt so that most materials are clearly presentable on smaller screens. Above all, keep it simple:

PDF files are the best format for large text files.

YouTube or Vimeo videos are viewable on smartphones as well as tablets. You can also upload audio files via YouTube or Vimeo. Slide presentations can be converted to video presentations with audio narration. They can also be published on YouTube or Vimeo.

Review your course carefully and put yourself in the shoes of the students. Would you be able to access every part of the course easily if you were depending on a smartphone?

 Course material is portable (e.g. text can be downloaded or printed out, material is well designed for handheld devices).

4.8 Resources

- Brown, T. (2003) Screen typefaces. Retrieved from: http://adminstaff.vassar.edu/tibrown/thesis/screenfaces.html.

- Lidwell, W., Holden, K., & Butler, J. (2003) *Universal Principles of Design: 125 Ways to Influence Perception, Increase Appeal, Make Better Design Decisions, and Teach through Design*. Beverly, MA: Rockport Publishers.

- Lynch, P.J. & Horton, S. (2006) Access by design: Design simply. Retrieved from: http://universalusability.com/access_by_design/fundamentals/simply.html.

- Lynch, P.J. & Horton, S. (2011) Web style guide online: Typography. Retrieved from: www.webstyleguide.com/wsg3/8-typography/.

 to do

While websites are more complex and visual than online courses, they are online and, as such, can help you review some basic principles of online design. Compare the following sets of competitive websites in terms of the design principles laid out here and the use of media covered in the chapter. Your main concern in reviewing them is usability:

- What is the purpose of the website?

- Is it easy to sort out—can you find what you need?

- Is all the text easily readable?

- Is it attractive—do you want to be there?

Compare the following with each other within these sets:

- www.aol.com, www.bing.com, www.google.com, www.yahoo.com

- www.guardianweekly.co.uk, www.nytimes.com, www.thestar.com

- www.apple.com, www.samsung.com, www.hp.com

- www.adobe.com, www.microsoft.com, www.oracle.com

- www.arts.ac.uk, www.fitnyc.edu, www.nas.edu.au, www.ocad.ca

- www.hbs.edu, www.london.edu, www.wharton.upenn.edu

You can do more comparisons in areas that interest you.

- Medina, J. (2014) *Brain Rules*. Seattle, WA: Pear Press.

- Motive Guides (2008) Web typography. Retrieved from: www.motive.co.nz/guides/typography/webfonts.php.

4.9 Summary and Standards

Using the standards of good, clear visual design elements can just become habit if you pay attention to them in the early stages of writing.

Again, the focus here is on simplicity, clarity, and openness. There should be nothing in the design of the page that distracts from communication. On the contrary, an open, clear, attractive page design enhances communication.

Look at Figures 4.3 and 4.4 again. Although visual enhancements have been added, none of this distracts or detracts. White space, bold and italic fonts, and different typefaces and type sizes are used purposefully to make distinctions, emphasize, and enhance readability, comprehension, and learning.

Layout

☐ Page layout is uncluttered and open, and includes a significant amount of white space.

☐ There is sufficient space between lines, paragraphs, and to the right and left of text so that it stands out and is easy to read.

☐ Text is left-justified and right margins are ragged.

☐ Headings and subheadings are used consistently to logically organize content.

Text

☐ A universal sans serif Web typeface (e.g. Verdana) assures access across platforms and enhances screen readability.

☐ Type size should be large enough to be easily readable by all students.

☐ Bold and italic typefaces are used sparingly only to emphasize important items.

☐ Underlining is used only for links.

☐ Words in all caps are avoided.

Color

☐ Color is used with purpose.

☐ There is good contrast between text and background.

Graphic Elements

☐ Visual elements (e.g. icons, shading, and color) are used consistently to distinguish between different types of course elements (e.g. lessons, assignments, audio, and video).

☐ Use bullets or numbers to set apart items that can be listed.

☐ Numbers are used to identify sequential steps in a task or process. They are also used for rankings and setting priorities.

☐ Bullets are used to highlight a series of items that are not prioritized or sequential.

☐ Content is designed simply and clearly to avoid information overload (e.g. avoid narrating while written text is visible, using distracting images for decoration, presenting too much information at once, etc.).

☐ Avoid combining spoken and written narrative in presentations.

Media

☐ Course material is portable (e.g. text can be downloaded or printed out, material is well designed for handheld devices).

☐ Videos should be no longer than 10 minutes in length.

Chapter 5 Engaging the Online Learner

Here are a variety of quotes to prepare you for this chapter:

> For the things we have to learn before we can do them, we learn by doing them.
>
> —Aristotle

> Knowledge is to be acquired only by a corresponding experience. How can we know what we are told merely?
>
> —Henry David Thoreau

> Give the pupils something to do, not something to learn; and the doing is of such a nature as to demand thinking; learning naturally results.
>
> —John Dewey

> Learning is not a spectator sport. Students do not learn much just by sitting in classes listening to teachers, memorizing prepackaged assignments and spitting out answers. They must talk about what they are learning, write about it, relate it to past experiences and apply it to their daily lives. They must make what they learn part of themselves.
>
> (Chickering & Gamson, 1987)

Three nights a week, Paul comes home from work, eats, then works on his online course. He stares at the screen, slowly scrolling and reading through the dense text. The "lecture" was written by a teacher hundreds of miles away. Paul studies online because this is the only way he can finish his degree and move on to better work opportunities.

Although he has contact with the teacher and the students through online text-based discussions, these, like the teacher's "lectures," are long and tedious.

He finds studying online an isolating experience, and it all takes more time than he counted on. Sometimes, he thinks he will just drop out, but his desire to improve his life keeps him motivated, so he carries on in spite of the mental drudgery.

Paul's teacher is required to teach this course online. She has done her best to recreate her lectures in written form, but just feels that it's not the same. There is no spontaneity. It can be challenging to make the subject matter interesting in a classroom setting, but online it just doesn't seem to work at all. She misses the contact with the students. The online text discussions do not engage the students in the way that she would like. She doesn't feel good about the experience in general. Her dropout rate is higher online than it is on-site.

The story above presents the classic negative image of online teaching and learning. We are here to show you that online learning can be involving, interesting, interactive, and social—in other words, engaging.

5.1 Teaching Components

There are essentially three components to online teaching. These are designed in advance of teaching the course:

- presentation—introduces new knowledge and skills;

- activities—provides opportunities for learning; and

- assessment and feedback.

note

Any time you need a reference point for an online course or learning management system, refer to the Chapter 2 tour for a complete example.

All of these components can and should be engaging. In fact, while activities will sometimes stand on their own, they will be part of well-designed presentations and assessments as well.

Active and engaging online courses are:

- **Clearly and attractively presented.** The material is inviting and openly displayed. There are no barriers to understanding. A variety of different modes (e.g. audio, text, video, images, hands-on) capture the interest and imaginations of learners.

- **Active and hands-on.** The material requires that learners are not only reading, listening, or watching, but doing something. This approach to teaching and learning emphasizes the critical importance of learners taking control of their own learning (Scardamalia & Bereiter, 1991). That is, they are active participants in the learning process. The teacher plays a central role in constructing experiences for engaging the learners. This can help raise student awareness and understanding of where they are in the learning process.

- **Authentic and meaningful.** The material is authentic, and/or comes close to real-world circumstances. It is true to its desired outcome. When a skill is being taught, learners can see the relationship between what they are doing in the course and its real-world application. Course curriculum should, to some extent, be flexible enough to draw on student prior knowledge to promote deep and meaningful learning.

- **Collaborative.** Learning is seen as a social experience. The learners feel responsible for their own learning. They contribute to others' learning. Contact with other learners and the teacher is easily accessible and continual. The learning environment promotes cooperation and sharing of perspectives. This leads students to develop multiple viewpoints and think critically. This also creates community.

- **Reflective.** The material encourages self-observation. It also helps students retrieve material that they may already know about the topic. There is time and opportunity to reflect built into the course. Self-assessments keep learners tuned in to where they are in the learning process.

- **Responsive to different degrees of a variety of student learning abilities and preferences.** For example, there is recognition of the learning preferences of intrapersonal learners, as well as interpersonal learners (see Figure 5.1). Hands-on, visual, logical, and linguistic learners are all considered.

We will look at the qualities of engaged learning in more detail as we move through the development of the components that make up an online course.

5.2 Student Learning Abilities/Preferences

[O]nce we realize that people have very different kinds of minds, different kinds of strengths—some people are good in thinking spatially, some in thinking language, others are very logical, other people need to be hands on and explore actively and try things out—then education, which treats everybody the same way, is actually the most unfair education. Because it picks out one kind of mind, which I call the law professor mind—somebody who's very linguistic and logical—and says, if you think like that, great, if you don't think like that, there's no room on the train for you.

(Edutopia, 1997); interview with Howard Gardner

 Go to the website for a brief article on Gardner's work with multiple intelligences.

Howard Gardner, a Harvard University education professor, published his landmark book, *Frames of Mind: The Theory of Multiple Intelligences*, in 1983. Gardner's work has resonated with many educators. It was an exciting revelation and has transformed what we know about learning. While many college and adult educators embrace the concept of addressing the variety in the way people learn, many fewer do it than should. Both this book and the book's website model an approach that focuses on a variety of learning abilities/preferences.

When following a purely textual model, online study emphasizes only linguistic intelligence. Visual learners, for example, may need visual elements (images, illustrations, graphs, video, etc.) that support content to do their best. These same visual elements support the learners that are not dependent on visual elements because in today's online world, we depend more and more on visual stimulation to communicate.

Some learners need active, hands-on engagement to do their best. Online learning can be a rather solitary experience,

An intrapersonal learner:	An interpersonal learner:
• needs to spend time alone to think and reflect	• is thought of as a good advisor
• is strong-willed and independent	• prefers to talk out problems and work with others rather than alone
• can spend days at a time alone	• enjoys teaching others
• thinks about life and the future	• feels comfortable in a crowd
• keeps a personal journal	• prefers playing games with others rather than alone

Figure 5.1 A comparison of interpersonal and intrapersonal learners

 to do

The chances are a learner will not be a linguistic or visual learner per se, but they will be stronger in some learning abilities than others.

 Why not take the VARK test? While it doesn't cover all of Gardner's intelligences, it will give you a good idea of how his ideas play out: http://vark-learn.com.

Once you have a sense of your strongest learning abilities, look at some websites. Which address your learning style? Which do not? How does the design of websites affect your attitude and willingness to spend time visiting them?

Now, look through this book and its website. We have tried to address a variety of learning preferences. Are you comfortable with the way the content is presented? Imagine you are someone with a complementary learning style to yours. Would you now be comfortable with the way information is presented? What have we done to make this information appeal to a range of learning preferences? What haven't we done? How do you respond to the presentation of information in this book as compared to a book that is mostly smaller type and fewer illustrations and visual examples? How does this relate to online learning?

perhaps appealing to the intrapersonal learner. Planning for collaboration and active learning, and incorporating outside resources, addresses interpersonal and kinesthetic (hands-on/physically engaged) learning.

It can be relatively easy to incorporate a variety of media and approaches into an online learning environment as compared to an on-site class. Access to the technology that facilitates this is a given. This variety of communicative approaches makes the course engaging for all learners.

☑ Presentations, activities, and assessments address a variety of learning abilities and preferences.

5.3 Roles of Participants in an Engaged Learning Process

Online course activities are more engaging when both teacher and learner participate in the learning process.

Teacher's Role

The teacher is just as engaged as the learners in online activities. She guides learners through the process of discovery, understanding, and knowledge construction. As facilitator and/or guide, the teacher helps learners recognize their goals and work toward achieving them. That is, the teacher takes on the perspective of the learner and provides feedback along with anticipating common issues and challenges (Hattie & Yates, 2014). Students bring in new information and experiences alongside the teacher. She often finds that she is learning alongside the learners.

☑ The teacher is a participant in the learning process.

Reflection

The Relationship between Online Course Design and Teaching

An online course *design* can set the stage for engagement. However, the actual engagement happens as students and teachers participate in the online course together.

When a teacher *designs* an online course, the content and chosen activities convey his understanding and point of view about the subject. But the course design does not replace a teacher's participation. Teachers bring their mastery of subject and maturity of experience to the interaction. They help students make connections to ideas and information that lie beyond the preconceived curriculum. A well-designed online course creates many opportunities for such responsive instruction.

How to *teach* an engaging online course has its own set of skills and considerations. Active participation, effective classroom management, responsive instruction, and timely pacing are all essential teaching skills that play out in new ways online. Online teaching strategies are the subject of the next book in this Routledge series, *Essentials of Online Teaching: A Standards-Based Guide* (2016).

Margaret McCabe, coauthor of *Essentials of Online Teaching: A Standards-Based Guide*

The Role of the Learner

Engaged learners are active participants in the learning process. They are responsible for their own learning and frequently contribute to others' learning. As active participants, learners explore, and are encouraged to construct, their own understandings of knowledge. They interact with the material, the technology, real-world situations, and others in the course to develop their understandings. The specific roles will change depending upon whether they are working alone, in pairs, in groups, or as a class.

Personal Perspective

Scott Thornbury

Experience has taught me that I teach better when I am also learning. For example, I'm a better language teacher when I'm also a language learner. And I'm a better teacher trainer when I, in turn, am learning a new skill.

Hence, my years working on the online program at The New School has been extraordinarily formative—the experience of learning how to exploit the available technologies in order to create a vibrant learning community has, I think, informed and improved my teaching—not just in this program, but whenever I have to face a new group of learners. I hope my students share some of this excitement!

Scott Thornbury lives in Barcelona. He designed and teaches two courses in the MA in Teaching English to Speakers of Other Languages at The New School in New York City.

Scott's examples in this book come from a course on Language Analysis for Teachers: Phonology/Lexis/Syntax (first taught at The New School). The textbook Scott uses, his own *About Language*, provides most of the activities for the course. To complement this, his online learners spend a fair amount of time working through online, interactive presentations that introduce, support, and reinforce the content (see Chapter 10).

Online learning may be novel to some learners. Therefore, we recommend that the teacher advises learners about the levels of interaction and communication required in both group and individual work, and suggestions for managing their time. This is critical when the course is designed based on students working together and reviewing their work products.

☑ **Learners take responsibility for their learning and, at times, the learning of others.**

Active learning simply means the learners are "doing." Doing includes writing, discussing, asking, questioning, critiquing, and collaborating. For more detail, refer to the use of verbs in the learning outcomes in Appendix A.

The Role of the Learner as a Member of a Group

Learning is a social process (Dewey, 1938); learners are in a class with others, including peers and teachers. Grouping learners together facilitates the sharing of multiple viewpoints and perspectives. Group members may present different viewpoints that reflect background (cultural, geographic, ethnic, socioeconomic), belief (political, religious), and/or experiences (professional, community, educational), which may influence others' perspectives and thinking. The group setting challenges learners to think beyond themselves and their subjective understandings of the world. Roles change according to how people work. Roles will also change depending upon the part the teacher plays (e.g. mediator, organizer, recorder, researcher, presenter, etc.).

The Role of the Learner Working in Pairs

Pairing learners is another form of grouping, where the exchanges between two learners are more productive than they would be in a larger group setting. Learners may work in pairs for specific types of assignments. In certain skills areas (e.g. languages, math, writing), they can reinforce each other's work more efficiently than when working in a larger group. When pairing learners, they should be rotated more frequently than in the group setting, so they are exposed to a range of skills and knowledge levels.

The Role of the Learner Working Alone

The intrapersonal learner needs to have the opportunity to work alone. This type of learner is engaged through activities that can be completed independently. Give learners ample opportunities to work alone. On the other hand, it is of great benefit to intrapersonal learners to learn to work with others to prepare them for collaborative experiences they may face in the world beyond their studies. The converse is true for interpersonal learners.

The Role of the Learner as a Member of a Community

Finally, the learner has a role as a member of the class community, relating to the class as a whole, as well as to the teacher. These roles are supported through development of content in a variety of formats. Class participation in discussion forums plays the dominant role in providing learner-to-class interaction.

- ☑ Students work in a variety of independent and collaborative configurations that reflect real-world situations.

- ☑ Class participation activities (e.g. discussion boards, wikis, social networks) are used to build community.

5.4 Collaborative Learning

> In the long history of humankind (and animal kind, too) those who learned to collaborate and improvise most effectively have prevailed.
>
> —Charles Darwin

Communication and collaboration with others support active, engaged learning and community. Collaborative group work is learner-centered. It requires that all members of the group actively participate. They are then responsible for their own learning and, in part, the learning of others.

Collaboration encourages the sharing of information and perspectives, and requires both independent responsibility and cooperation. For example, a learner may be required to work as a member of a team, or in pairs. In many cases, collaboration reflects the realities of working under real-world conditions, where individuals may typically work in teams.

Types of Groups

Learners are encouraged to interact with others (fellow classmates, guest experts and practitioners, the instructor, and outside sources) and benefit from their experience and expertise (see also Group Projects in Section 6.5).

Different types of activities require different ways to group learners. Here are three common grouping techniques:

1. **Heterogeneous groups.** Learners are grouped by their differences in skills and/or knowledge. For example, each learner in the group may have a different skill critical to the success of the group activity.

2. **Homogeneous groups.** Learners are grouped by their similarities in knowledge, skills, or simply by the group's unique task. For example, if you wanted to hold an online debate for or against an issue, the two sides should be fairly well matched.

3. **Jigsaw groups.** The jigsaw method is commonly used to have learners work cooperatively. Each group member is assigned a unique task. The goal is for the learners to present their findings to one another. To ensure the findings are accurate, learners consult with members of other groups assigned with the same task.

 For more details on how jigsaw groups work, see www.jigsaw.org.

The point is that you probably want to group learners in a thoughtful and appropriate way that draws upon the experience, knowledge, and skills of the students, rather than just randomly. The size of the grouping should be appropriate to the task.

Preparing for Collaboration

When designing and planning for collaborative learning in your course:

- create a safe and supportive culture;

- provide guidelines and expectations for group activities;

- indicate the responsibilities and roles of the students; and

- build in a way for learners to assess one another's performance working in the group.

Review the strategies for grouping learners for collaborative activities. Begin thinking about the following:

- Which of the following is most appropriate for the subject area you are teaching:
    - small groups, 3–4?
    - large groups, 6–8?
    - whole class?
    - pairs?
    - individuals?

- Think about how to group students (see page 88).

- What is the teacher's role?

- What will be the product or outcome of their work?

Most LMSs provide spaces for groups of learners to collaborate and communicate. Simple tools such as Google Docs are also good for collaboration and give students experience with the tools used in many workplaces.

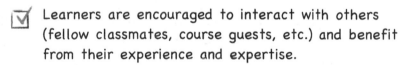 **Learners are encouraged to interact with others (fellow classmates, course guests, etc.) and benefit from their experience and expertise.**

Collaborative activities are designed to facilitate a safe learning environment.

Procedures for group activities are specified so that students are aware of their role and responsibility in collaborative activities.

Personal Perspective

Kristen Sosulski

I assign a lot of group work in my online courses. I teach in a business school so it's important to simulate authentic work activities such as a team working on a presentation for the board of directors.

Students studying online can benefit from working together in teams. In the workplace, teams collaborate across geographic locations; this is true for online coursework as well. While my students may be studying abroad or in New York City, I provide them with tools for team collaboration. I particularly encourage (but never require) online real-time meetings for online teams. Some of the free tools I recommend are Skype, Google Hangouts, and Google Docs.

5.5 Summary and Standards

In this chapter, we have introduced you to the key characteristics of engaged learning. Engaged learning requires that students are actively engaged in the process. It's simple really—when both teacher and learner collaborate in the learning process, online activities are more engaging.

- [ ] Presentations, activities, and assessments address a variety of learning abilities and preferences.

- [ ] The teacher is a participant in the learning process.

- [ ] Learners take responsibility for their learning and, at times, the learning of others.

- [ ] Students work in a variety of independent and collaborative configurations that reflect real-world situations.

- [ ] Class participation activities (e.g. discussion boards, wikis, social networks) are used to build community.

☐ Learners are encouraged to interact with others (fellow classmates, course guests, etc.) and benefit from their experience and expertise.

☐ Collaborative activities are designed to facilitate a safe learning environment.

☐ Procedures for group activities are specified so that students are aware of their role and responsibility in collaborative activities.

Chapter 6

Activities and Tools: Working Collaboratively and Independently

This chapter introduces an essential variety of adaptable activities that can be used across a range of fields and types of students. What can be done with this collection is limited only by the imagination, experience, and problem-solving skills of the teacher/designer.

Above all, activities must support the learning outcomes of the course. The quality of the learning experience depends on what activities you use, and how engaging the activities are for the students. Students should be frequently engaged in activities throughout the course.

We cover **six basic types of online activities** that work well across a range of subjects and the tools that support them, including social media platforms (see Table 6.1). Most experienced teachers have come up with a repertoire of activity setups that either fit into the activities we have discussed or can just be redesigned for an online course.

These activity types and variations are designed to address thinking skills and encourage active learning, collaboration, and class communication. We'll begin with the productive activities, then reflective activities, and finally introduce some examples of receptive activities.

Activities and Tools

Table 6.1 Online activity types and tools

Type of Activity	Tool	Variation	Participants
Class Discussion	Discussion forum Social media (Twitter, Facebook, LinkedIn)	• Building a class community • Questions and answers • Weekly topic discussions	Pairs to full classes
Journal Writing	Blog	• Individual reflections • Teacher reflections/ modeling	Individuals
Shared Knowledge Base	Wiki, Google Groups, Facebook Groups, etc.	• Collaborative glossary • Annotated bibliography	Group to class
Practice Exercises and Self-Assessments	Testing/quizzing with feedback features	• Multiple-choice • Fill-in-the-blank • Gap-fill • Drag and drop • Matching • True and false • Short answer • Self-graded exercises	Individuals to pairs
Projects	Multiple options, such as workgroups, wikis, blogs, YouTube, Vimeo, and common presentation tools (e.g. PowerPoint)	• Group project presentations • Group research projects	Individuals to pairs to class
Receptive Activities	PDFs, podcasts Here, students are the receivers of the student projects so many are the same tools as above	• Teacher/student audio/visual presentations • Course readings • Miscellaneous audio and video of demonstrations, lectures, etc.	Individuals
Research	Internet searches, online databases via university and college libraries such as ProQuest and Omni Wilson	• Literature reviews, meta-analyses, reports • Peer reviews of research reports, video presentation of secondary research findings • Primary research such as interviews	Individuals to pairs

☑ Activities are frequent and varied. Students may respond to questions, select options, provide information, or interact with others.

☑ Activities engage students in higher-level thinking skills, including critical and creative thinking, analysis, and problem-solving.

☑ Course content is designed to encourage interactions between learners.

☑ Resources and activities support learning outcomes.

6.1 Class Participation and Discussions

Online class discussions facilitate student–class participation in an online course.

Types of Discussion Activities

There are many ways to create dynamic and rich class discussions, either formal or informal, in an online course. Shaul (2007) identifies three discussion forum types:

- social;

- general; and

- topic-driven.

For each type, the goal is to create a space that encourages discussion and community. Three small discussion activities are presented below. We encourage you to use all three when designing the course.

DISCUSSION BOARD

Online Class Discussion

What?

Online discussions in an asynchronous environment are set up as written "conversations." The entire class participates. See Figure 6.1 for an example of a simple discussion forum called "Introduce Yourself."

The content and goals of the activity dictate the appropriate configuration. One can easily upload images, link to websites, and embed audio and video segments in your discussion posts.

Why?

Discussion is a core activity in any class, online or on-site. Very often, the discussion forum is the central place where class members get together to communicate. It is often at the core of the learning process and participation is usually required at least two to three times a week.

Where?

All LMSs provide a communication tool for discussion, known as a discussion forum, a forum, a discussion board, or a bulletin board. Discussion forums vary in their design, functionality, and setup; however, they all have certain characteristics in common.

Who?

Pairs to groups to whole class including the teacher.

How?

1. The teacher sets up the topic by **creating a forum in the discussion board for the entire class or specific groups**. This may be a question to the class or a topic for conversation (e.g. Introduce Yourself, Q&A, etc.). **Each forum has a topic title and topic posting** (see Figure 6.2).
2. Learners reply to the forum topic posed by the teacher. Each reply (thread) contains a subject related to the topic, and a message (the response). The student's subject may be Clyde's Introduction (see Figure 6.2). The message is the actual student introduction written in text form. Class members (both students and teacher) reply to each other's threads (see Figure 6.3).

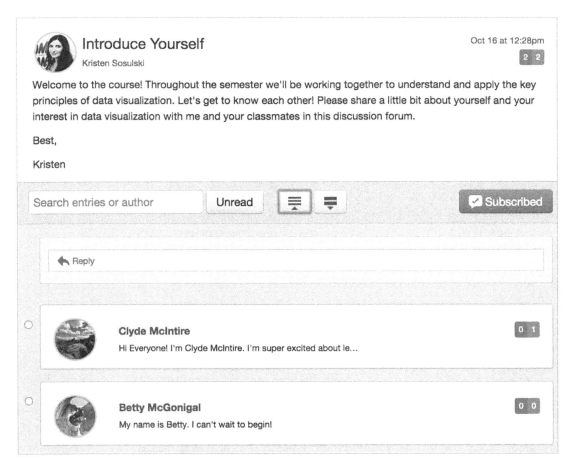

Figure 6.1 An example of a threaded discussion forum from Kristen's course, prompting class members to post an introduction of themselves. When the message title above is clicked on, it opens the full message (see Figure 6.2).

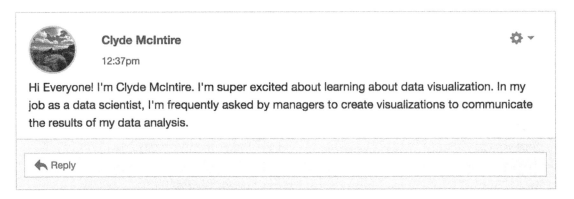

Figure 6.2 A reply posted by a student introducing himself to the class

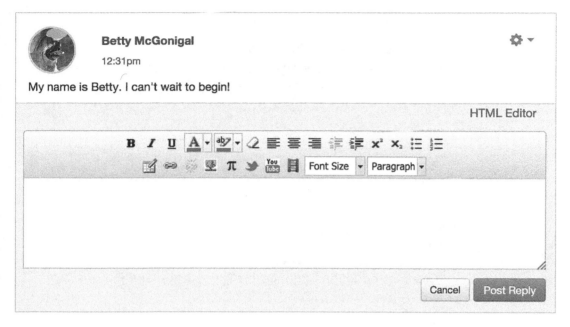

Figure 6.3 The reply message window

Discussion Board—Variation

Online Class Discussion—Introduce Yourself

The "Introduce Yourself" discussion forum has the following advantages in an online course. It:

- allows the teacher and learners to get to know one another;
- allows for the possibility of extending their relationships into another social forum such as the class cafe;
- provides an introduction and practice on using the forums in the online course; and
- enables the teacher to identify learners with similar interests, which may inform how the teacher groups learners for collaborative work later on in the course.

See Figure 6.1 for an example of creating an introductory activity where all students introduce themselves and share their interests.

Activity: Social Forums—Building a Class Community

During the early part of an online course, it is critical for class members to get to know one another, and begin to build an online class community. Building community is essential for building a successful online course.

The teacher also participates in the online activity. For example, the teacher can also post her introduction as a thread. Of course, she will respond to the students' threads as they unfold.

Below are some ideas for topics that encourage rapport-building:

- Class introductions and ice-breaking tasks (see Figures 6.2, 6.3, and 6.4).

- Student meetings. Students can arrange "face-to-face" or online live Web conference meetings. They can then report back to the class as a whole.

- Social network groups.

- Online "class cafe." This is an open, ongoing forum where students talk with classmates. They share topics of interest such as recent news articles, career opportunities, etc. This is similar to students meeting in a real cafe during course breaks.

☑ Online spaces (e.g. discussion boards, social networks) are in place for students to participate in and meet outside the class.

tip

For a Q&A to be successful, the teacher should encourage the class to respond to each other's questions. This can save the teacher and students time.

Activity: Social Forums—Icebreaker

> An ice-breaker should not require anything more than the ability to express knowledge of self. It relates more to the personal life than to the academic life of the learner.
>
> (Conrad & Donaldson, 2004, p. 47)

Salmon (2002), in her book *E-tivities*, provides examples of online icebreakers. Our favorite examples include a "Quiz of all the class members."

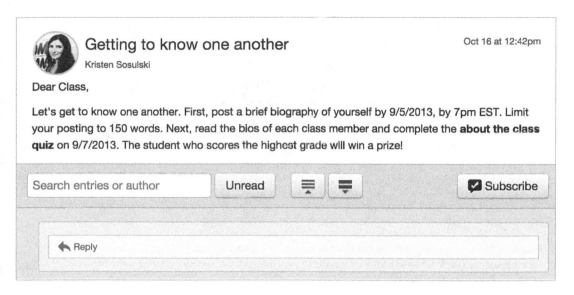

Figure 6.4 An online icebreaker (adapted from Salmon, 2002)

In this icebreaker, the teacher asks all the students to post some information about themselves. After each student has contributed, the teacher can set up a quiz that tests the students' knowledge of each class member. See Figure 6.4 for an example of the first part of the icebreaker activity. After students post their biography to the discussion forum, they are directed to read the biographies of the other students. Finally, students take an online quiz that is set up more like a contest to test their knowledge of their fellow classmates. The highest scorer is rewarded with a prize such as extra credit on an assignment.

Activity: General Forums—Question and Answer (Q&A)

When online learners have a question, there are two ways to have them ask it:

- Email the question directly to the teacher as a private communication.

- Post the question in a discussion forum as a public communication to the class.

The drawback of the email approach is that the learner is relying on the teacher as the sole provider of information. Instead, set up a Q&A discussion forum for the duration of the online course (see Figures 2.10 and 6.5). This saves time for the teacher and encourages communication. Be sure to include this in your communication strategies section in the syllabus (see Chapters 2 and 9).

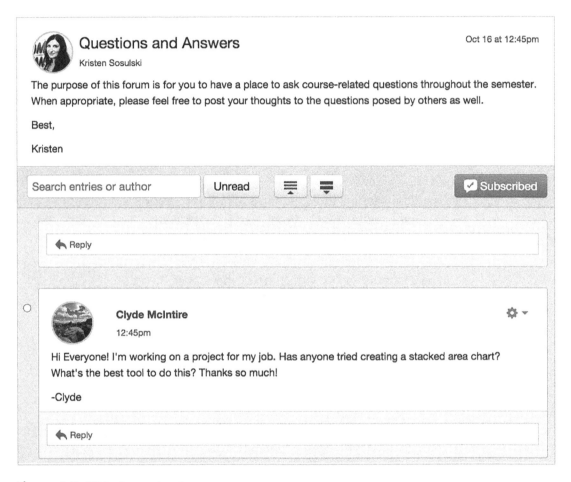

Figure 6.5 Q&A discussion forum

Online Class Discussion—Question and Answer

 In an online course, the Q&A discussion forum has the following advantages:

- It provides a single, convenient place for learners to ask administrative questions related to assignments, due dates, and requirements.
- A student's questions are made public to the class. This is similar to a student raising her hand in an on-site class. Everyone gets to see the question. The teacher has to respond only once to the question and all students will benefit from learning the new information the response provides.
- It encourages community-building within the course. Students are encouraged to help others by posting their thoughts on the question. This supports a student-centered approach.

Figure 6.5 is an example of a Q&A discussion forum. Notice how the teacher keeps the purpose of the forum brief and encourages other learners to respond when they feel it is appropriate.

Online Class Discussion—Content Discussions

The "content-based discussion forum" has the following characteristics. It:

- provides a place for asking questions about and discussing a new topic;
- designates a place for learners to explore the topic with others and clarify their understanding of the weekly course content; and
- enables students to analyze and synthesize class readings and observations through a focused exchange of ideas.

Figure 6.6 is an example of a topic-based discussion. Notice how the students are replying to one another, not just to the teacher.

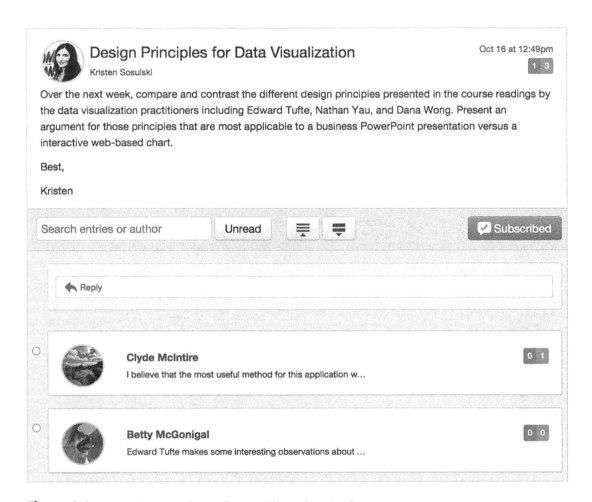

Figure 6.6 A topic-based discussion activity using the forum

Activity: Topic-Driven Forums—Weekly Content Discussions

As discussed throughout this book, **class participation is critical in an online class**. Topic-driven forums encourage and facilitate discussion of course topics. These forums usually focus on a single topic for a defined period of time.

Weekly topic-based discussions are the equivalent of classroom discussions in an on-site class. Once forum content is presented, this is where the class goes to discuss it. Typically, student discussion is tied to the class participation grade. This ensures active class discussion.

One of the benefits of this asynchronous discussion is that students can reflect and think about their responses rather than having to respond immediately, as is typical in an on-site class. Also, each and every student must respond. In an on-site class, this is usually not the case. Then, the teacher can provide feedback to the class as a whole, highlighting the salient points from the discussion and areas for improvement. Feedback is communicated through a discussion forum posting or a class announcement.

tip

Be sure that the questions you pose inspire conversation and discussion. Avoid yes/no questions and those that can be answered with only one or two words.

6.2 Online Journaling Activities

Types of Online Journaling Activities

The variance in types of journals relates to what the teacher, as guide, emphasizes and what the student prefers. This has a great deal to do with who is reading the journal: one person, a small group, or the whole class.

Students may not want to share reflective work with anyone but the teacher. When this is the case, what benefits the student most should determine the outcome. **The goal in this case is that the students develop the habit of reflecting on their work.** In order to do this, they must be comfortable with the process.

ONLINE JOURNALING

What?

The student keeps a log of written entries, organized chronologically by date or by topic. Similar to discussion forums, blogs are typically public (to the class), and therefore this is not a private activity. This allows the teacher (or the entire class) to view and comment on the student postings/entries throughout the course.

Why?

Online journaling is an activity that allows students to reflect on the steps they take to understand new knowledge or develop a new skill. This reflection can take many forms, such as critiquing class readings or logging progress on a project or research paper. Journaling is an individual activity that lets the teacher know what students are thinking about their own learning and development.

Where?

In a blog. A blog is short for weblog, or more simply, a running web page with multiple entries (articles, reflections, diary entries, etc.) that includes text, images, links to websites, audio, and/or video clips. Some LMSs have blogging as an option. If yours doesn't, try these popular blogging platforms: Blogger, Tumblr, and WordPress.

A simpler alternative (if you do not have access to a blog) allows students to post to a discussion forum instead. Set up a separate forum for each student. Create an online class rule in which only the "owner" of a forum can create threads, and one, some, or all others can reply (this is equivalent to commenting in a blog).

Who?

Individuals blogging with one or more class members reading and responding.

How?

1. **The teacher introduces the assignment.** The instructions include the teacher's assessment criteria for the blog posting and comments.
2. **The student posts an entry to his blog.** The student keeps a log of written entries, organized chronologically by date or by topic.

An entry is simply written text that may include images, video, and/or links (see Figure 6.7).

3. **The class members, including the teacher, leave comments** on each author's blog (see Figure 6.8).

4. **The blog author may also post comments back** to his own blog.

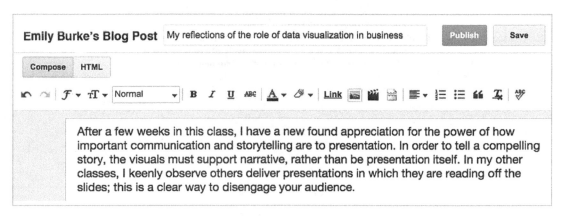

Figure 6.7 A blog posting in edit-mode

Activity: Individual Reflections via the Blog

tip

It's easy for students to post a response to the questions or topics posed by the teacher. Encourage students to reply to one another in your instructions and in the syllabus. Indicate that not doing so can affect their grade.

In an online course, there are several ways for the teacher to assess how well students understand assigned readings. One technique is for students to complete a reading and then reflect upon it afterwards. Students can summarize their interpretation of the reading and relate it to prior knowledge and understanding (see Figure 6.8). Or the teacher may post specific questions that require analysis of what has been read. While this often occurs in shared dialogue in the discussion board, journal writing may allow the students to express themselves more freely. The teacher provides feedback by posting a comment to the student blog. Teachers can also provide feedback on individual blog postings through email, if they do not want their comments to be seen by the entire class.

My reflections of the role of data visualization in business
by Emily Burke

After a few weeks in this class, I have a new found appreciation for the power of how important communication and storytelling are to presentation. In order to tell a compelling story, the visuals must support narrative, rather than be presentation itself. In my other classes, I keenly observe others deliver presentations in which they are reading off the slides; this is a clear way to disengage your audience.

Post a Comment

I share many of your same reflections.on the role of data visualization in business. The presenter is the important element in the presentation. The presenter is the presentation. Any materials such as charts, graphs, pictures, slides, movies, and animations should only support and enhance the presentation.

Comment as: Steven Ward ⬍   **Sign out**

Publish   Preview   ☐ Notify me

Figure 6.8 Adding a comment to a blog posting

Online Journaling—Variation

Teacher Reflections

 See the website for another take on using the blog as a place to post individual reflections.

Teachers share their reflections with the class and solicit comments. The teacher also serves as a model.

This is a great example of the teacher as a participant in the online course. This includes the main posting by the teacher and the comments/responses by students that are appended to the blog posting.

6.3 Shared Knowledge Base

> Wikis are flexible and intensely collaborative. They are administered by a number of people and can be organized in innumerable ways. If you want to engage in personal reflection, you use a blog, but if you want collaboration, you use a wiki.
>
> (Zeinstejer, 2008)

Types of Knowledge Base-Building Activities

Other online documents that can be created using a wiki include:

- class glossary;

- group research projects;

- class bibliographies and/or Web resources relevant to course topics;

- group or class projects;

- error corrections—language, facts, history, news, etc.;

- timelines/chronological lists;

- annotations for articles, poems, case studies, readings, etc. with multimedia and links; and

- group or class storyboards for film-, media-, technology-related subjects, etc.

note

Wikipedia (www.wikipedia.com) is an example of how a wiki is used to support ongoing contributions to an online encyclopedia. Unlike a physical encyclopedia, a wiki encyclopedia is not a static set of information. As new events occur, they are added to Wikipedia from the large online community of contributors.

SHARED KNOWLEDGE BASE

What?

The class/group is essentially building one or more documents together, online. Anyone who is given permission to work on the document can add, modify, and/or delete the contents. The authorship is shared. It is not just a reflection of one individual's participation and contribution. The content is always in progress and is thought of as growing and evolving.

Why?

Student collaboration builds community in an online class, enabling the co-creation of knowledge and products, and aiding in the development of critical thinking skills (Palloff & Pratt, 2005). Additionally, collaborative projects emphasize to students that the online course is not just interacting with the teacher, but with their peers as well.

Where?

In a wiki—a collaborative tool in which an online document is created that supports the inclusion of text, images, video and audio, and links to other documents. Wikis are quick "because the process of reading and editing is combined" (Lamb, 2004). If your LMS doesn't have a wiki, some popular wikis include PBwiki and Wikispaces, or even Google Docs.

Who?

Group to class—the authorship of a wiki is shared. There can be groups of students working on different projects or the whole class working on one.

How?

1. Teacher creates the wiki and enables the selected course members to edit it. Editing a wiki simply means adding to it and modifying it.
2. Teacher posts instructions for the assignment within the wiki document.
3. Students begin viewing, adding to, and modifying the content of the wiki.

Activity: Collaborative Glossary

When learners are taking a course in a new area of study that includes unfamiliar terminology, there are two ways to present information:

- the teacher defines it directly for the learner; or

- the learner identifies the terms he doesn't know and seeks out the definition.

What if the students collaborated on their own glossary?

Shared Knowledge Base—Variation

Collaborative Glossary

 Building a shared online glossary has the following advantages in an online course. It:

- creates good study habits;
- strengthens research skills;
- leads to a better understanding of concepts through close-up work and analysis;
- saves time for the teacher; and
- fosters collaboration skills.

To create an online collaborative glossary, you can use a **wiki**. Figure 6.9 is an example of the activity description by Heidi Wittford in her Globalization and Higher Education graduate course at NYU. The activity begins with the teacher posting a term and its definition.

Note: This activity requires oversight and feedback from the teacher to ensure definitions provided are accurate. The teacher can provide feedback through periodic course announcements highlighting the areas that need revision, further explanation, etc.

Wiki Assignment

This wiki will be a repository for an ongoing list of terms and definitions encountered in the readings and other course content. Since many of the terms encountered in the course content have multiple and contradictory definitions, keeping a running list will be helpful in sorting through complex and evolving definitions.

Figure 6.9 Teacher instructions for an online glossary-building activity

Activity: Collaborative Timeline/Chronological List

To give students a big-picture perspective, have them create a timeline or chronological list on an area of study. The area of study may be a field itself, such as a scientific or mathematical discipline, higher education, a religion, a branch of philosophy, etc. Or try something more specific, such as milestones in the history of a movement, including influences, developments, and events that affected its evolution.

6.4 Practice Exercises

While many of the practice exercise types described below are not usually seen as collaborative, they are interactive. Under the right circumstances, they can be a valuable addition to the work done in an online course. This is obviously true for certain kinds of skills classes such as languages and math.

PRACTICE EXERCISE

What?

A testing and quizzing setup provides a channel for learners to practice with teacher-designed exercises and self-assessments. The teacher can address many levels of thinking skills through the use of multiple choice, matching, drag-and-drop, true/false, fill-in-the-blank, and short-answer questions.

Why?

The benefit of using the testing tool is the instant feedback it can provide to students. However, the benefit is minimal if the testing tool cannot be adapted to be a practice exercise tool. That is, if the students do not have the opportunity to analyze incorrect or partially correct answers and keep trying to get to the best answer, then the tool is just constantly testing and does not itself help the students learn. By working through practice exercises, students have the opportunity to reach mastery of a skill or sets of information.

Where?

Most LMSs are equipped with a **Test Manager**. This is a great tool for organizing exercises, despite its use of the word "test." It enables the teacher to set up a "test" with questions and provide students with feedback on correct and incorrect answers. However, some LMSs may do better at enabling feedback than others.

There are stand-alone subject-specific programs available on the Web (e.g. Khan Academy covers a variety of subject areas). In addition, many major textbook publishers have created very good online chapter-by-chapter practice exercises and activities that complement and enhance their textbooks. Teachers can set up quizzes and exercises within these textbook websites and select from a pool of questions and question types, and customize when and how feedback is given to the learners. Furthermore, learner performance can be recorded for the teacher to review (for graded and practice tests and exercises).

Who?
Individuals and pairs.

How?

1. Begin by drafting the questions for the practice exercise.
2. Determine the grade percentage for the entire exercise and point value for each question.
3. Consider and craft the feedback that you would like to provide to students on their correct and incorrect answers. In some cases, the computer can correct. In others, you might add hints to wrong answers to get them to the correct answers. Ideally, the learners can keep trying until they get to a correct answer.
4. Build the test.
5. Make the test available to the students and set the time frame, if relevant.
6. Direct students to the practice exercise.
7. Students go to the designated place in the online course to complete the practice exercises.
8. The teacher provides feedback to short-answer questions. The computer provides the teacher-created feedback on those questions that are multiple-choice, true/false, fill-in-the-blank, and/or matching.

Types of Practice Exercises
Multiple Choice

Learners select their answers based on a finite set of options. The questions may have answers that are mutually exclusive or not. The answers are evaluated by a computer and may include automatic or teacher-created feedback (see Figure 6.10).

Figure 6.10 A multiple-choice exercise with corrections. Students have the opportunity to try question 2 again.

Source: English360 Web-based version of *Business Benchmark: Pre-Intermediate to Intermediate* BULATS Edition by Norman Whitby copyright Cambridge University Press

tip

If the program you are using only has a testing function without practice exercise features, it may help to have students work in pairs. The exercises then take on a problem-solving feature that may enhance learning.

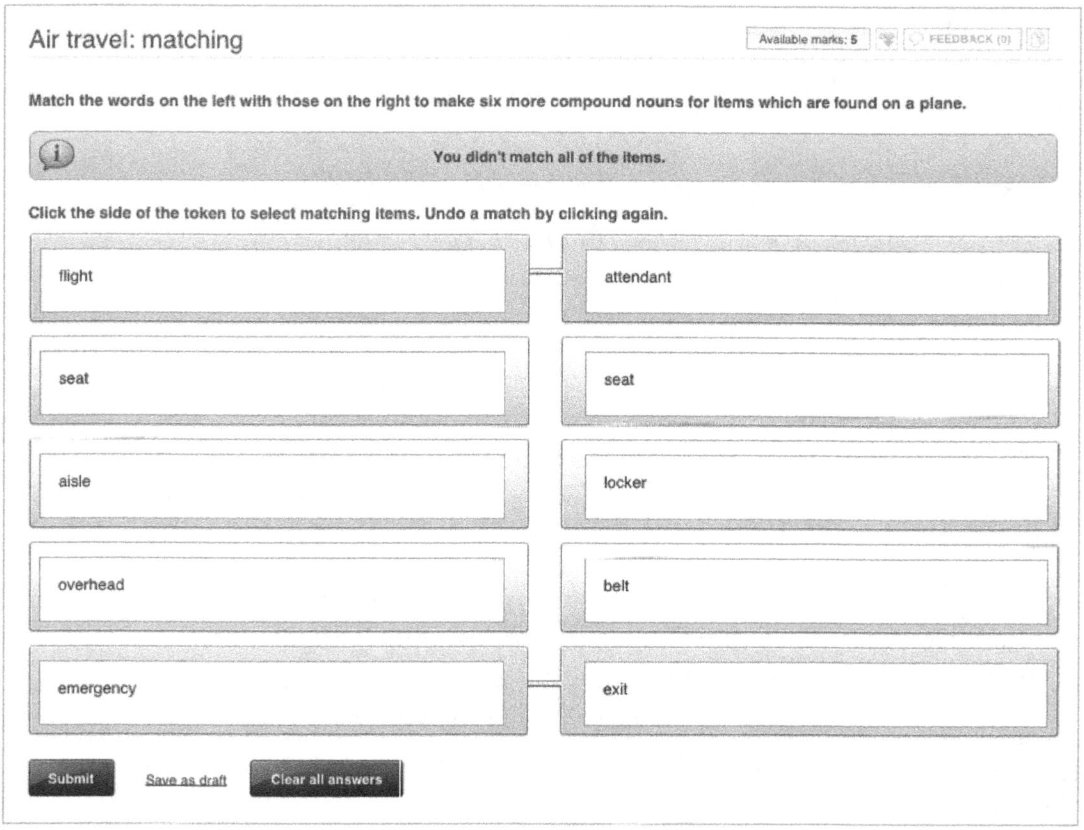

Matching

Students match an item in column A with an item in column B. The answers to matching question types can be evaluated on their computer (see Figure 6.11).

The student has chosen the matches he thinks are correct and the computer now shows which are incorrect. Ideally, the student can keep trying until all are correct (see Figure 6.12).

Figure 6.11 A gap-fill exercise where students drag their answers to the boxes

Source: English360 *English for Healthcare Professionals* by Virginia Allum

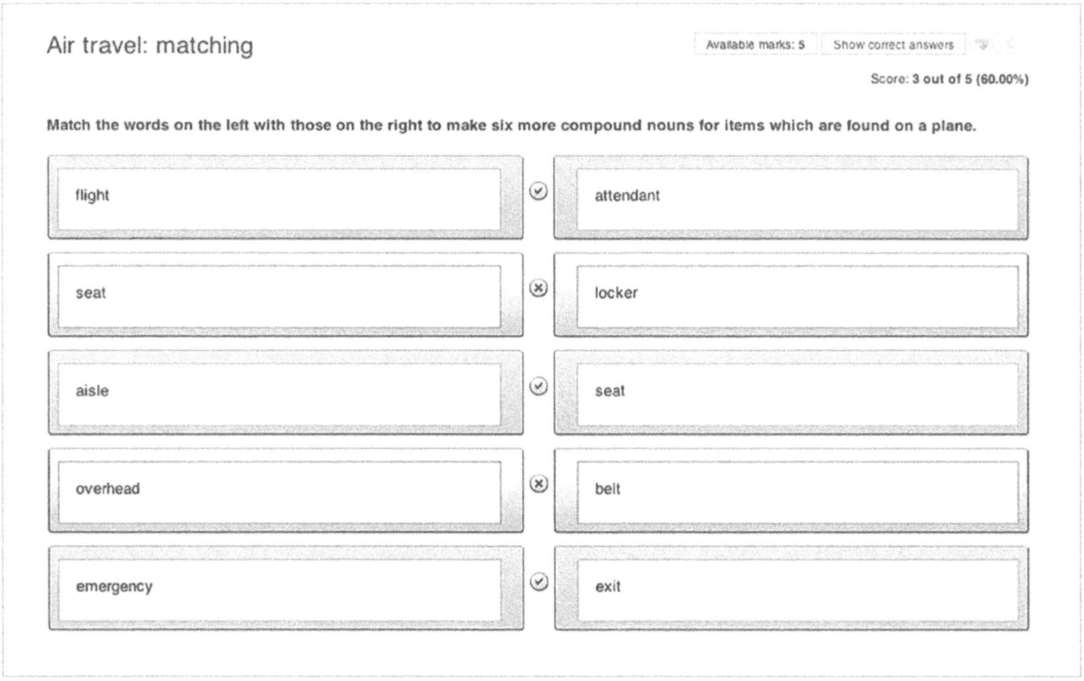

Figure 6.12 An online matching exercise

Source: English360 Web-based version of *Business Benchmark Pre-Intermediate to Intermediate* BULATS Edition by Norman Whitby copyright Cambridge University Press

Gap-Fill Exercise

Gap Fill
The term "gap fill" is British English (BE). Americans may not be familiar with the term. It is used to distinguish the exercise of providing the answers, which are then dragged to the blank, as opposed to a fill-in-the-blank exercise in which answers are typed in.

In a gap-fill exercise, students are given all of the possible answers. They drag each answer into the blank they think it belongs in.

Figures 6.13 and 6.14 show an online gap-fill/listening exercise using drag and drop. Students drag their answer from the right into one of the boxes on the left. The computer then corrects and allows students to try until they get all answers correct. In Figure 6.14, the incorrect answers have been removed so the student can try again. Finally, in Figure 6.15, the student has gotten all the answers in the right places.

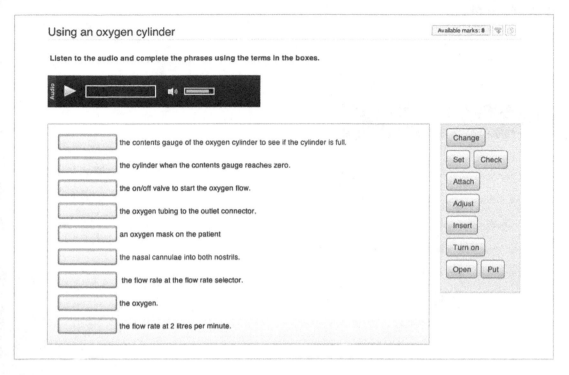

Figure 6.13 A gap-fill exercise where students drag their answers to the boxes

Source: English360 *English for Healthcare Professionals* by Virginia Allum

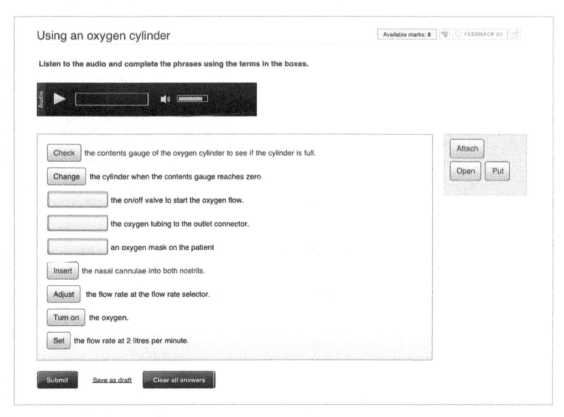

Figure 6.14 A gap-fill exercise with the correct and incorrect answers highlighted.

Source: English360 *English for Healthcare Professionals* by Virginia Allum

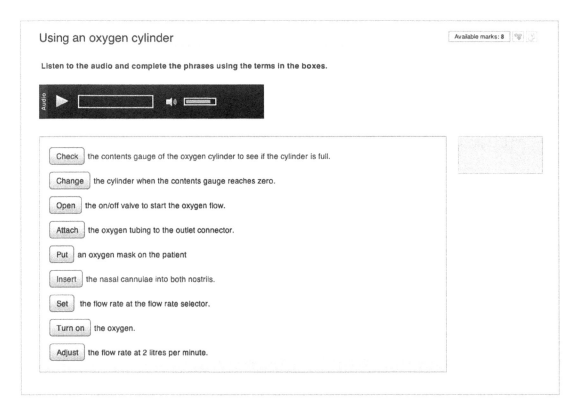

Figure 6.15 Gap fill with all answers correct

Fill-in-the-Blank

Students enter a word or a phrase to complete a statement (see Figure 6.16). The answers to fill-in-the-blank questions can be evaluated on their computer. However, often **responses from students must be an exact match.** For example, a misspelling would count as a wrong answer.

This can be frustrating to the student and may impede learning (e.g. in foreign languages). Use fill-in-the blank exercises sparingly and with care when they are computer-corrected.

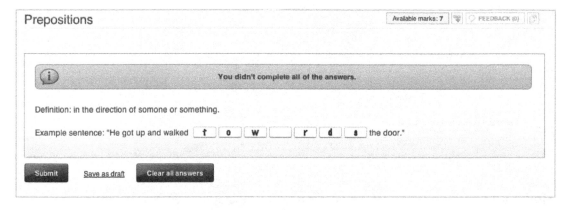

Prepositions   Available marks: 7   FEEDBACK (0)

Definition: in the direction of somone or something.

Example sentence: "He got up and walked [t] [o] [w] [o] [r] [d] [s] the door."

Figure 6.16 A gap-fill exercise with the answer typed in by the student

Source: self-authored task created using English360 authoring tools

In well-designed fill-ins, if any in a series of letters or words are correct and in the right order, the program will leave them as they are and only remove the incorrect elements (see Figure 6.17). This gives students something to build on when they are allowed to retry until they get to a better or right answer. In this case, the exercise truly becomes a learning experience and reinforcement of what they already know.

Figures 6.16 and 6.17 are set up to show how a very simple vocabulary fill-in might work.

Prepositions   Available marks: 7   FEEDBACK (0)

ⓘ   You didn't complete all of the answers.

Definition: in the direction of somone or something.

Example sentence: "He got up and walked [t] [o] [w] [ ] [r] [d] [s] the door."

Submit   Save as draft   Clear all answers

Figure 6.17 A gap-fill exercise with the incorrect letter removed. The student now has the opportunity to try again and type in the correct letter

Source: self-authored task created using English360 authoring tools

True/False

Students evaluate whether a statement or phrase is true or false. The answers to true/false questions can be evaluated on their computer. These are similar in design to multiple-choice questions. These can be designed with three choices where the third is "can't tell," or "doesn't say," for example.

A different kind of teacher

Available marks: 7   Show correct answers

Score: 2 out of 7 (28.57%)

Read the article about Linda Matthews and say if the sentences are 'Right', 'Wrong', or 'Doesn't say'.

Linda is a 40-year-old teacher based in London who loves her job. She works with children aged 6-12 but she doesn't teach in a school. She is a 'private tutor' - she goes to people's houses after school and helps young children with their homework. She teaches them English, French, Maths, Geography, History and Science. "I like working with one student at a time because I can really help him or her to get better. When you teach a big class, it's difficult to see what each student needs and you can't spend your time with only one child."

Linda has been a tutor for nearly 20 years now. Every afternoon she goes to one or two different houses and spends a few hours with a child. "I have to travel to a different part of London every day and sometimes there's a lot of traffic," Linda says. But she doesn't mind that. "One thing I don't like much about my job is when the parents get angry with their children if they don't get the best mark in class," she explains. "Most of my students work very hard through the year, but they get nervous about the exams. Their parents should understand that, but all they want are good marks."

1. Linda doesn't teach teenagers.
(✓) Right   ◯ Wrong   ◯ Doesn't say

2. Linda's students come to her house for lessons.
(✗) Right   ◯ Wrong   ◯ Doesn't say

3. Linda has never taught big classes.
◯ Right   ◯ Wrong   (✓) Doesn't say

Figure 6.18 A corrected true/false question type. The student can now try again to get item 2 correct. To do so she may decide to read the selection again to see what she missed

Source: English360 KEY practice task authored by Katie Foufouti for Laureate KSA Vocational progamme

Drag and Drop

Students can manipulate phrases or objects by dragging them around the screen and then dropping them where they think they belong (see Figure 6.19). This can be used for some of the above-mentioned purposes (gap-fill, matching), but also has other uses, such as having students categorize or organize items in defined ways.

In Figure 6.19, the answers have been corrected. Since there are only two boxes to choose from, getting the last two right will be easy. However, just the act of paying attention and moving the two words will aid with learning.

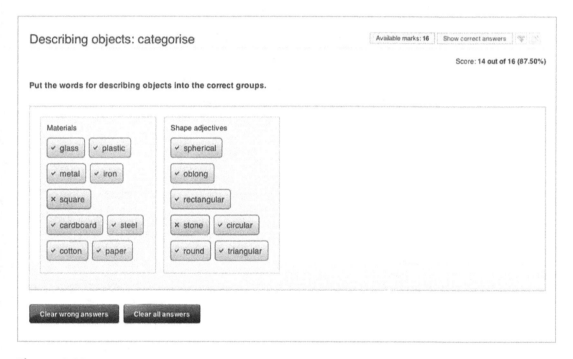

Figure 6.19 An example of a drag-and-drop categorization exercise. Students must drag each of the words into one of two category boxes.

Source: English360 Web-based version of *Business Benchmark: Pre-Intermediate to Intermediate* BULATS Edition by Norman Whitby copyright Cambridge University Press

Short Answer

Short-answer questions require feedback from the teacher and therefore require a time lag. The response, however, should get to the student in a timely fashion. Whether a test question or a practice exercise, short answers usually require a direct response from the teacher. This then requires a time lag. In a practice exercise, the teacher may respond to the student one or more times until the student gets the answer correct.

There are also immediate automated ways to respond to short-answer questions that require the teacher to enter responses ahead of time:

- The teacher may give students the correct answer when their answer is incorrect, and explain why it is correct.

- The teacher may refer to textbook or reference materials where the student can find the correct answer.

 While designing and building the actual practice exercise is time-consuming, in the long run this can save the instructor time by automating feedback to students.

Figure 6.20 An example of a short-answer question from a practice English language exercise. The student is typing his answer into the text box

Source: English360 *Crossing Cultures* by Valentina Dodge

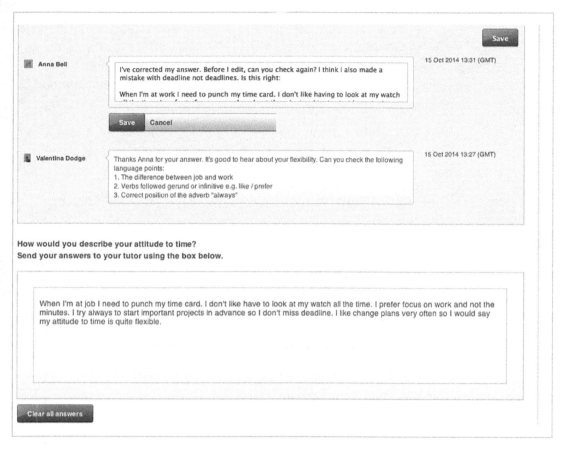

Figure 6.21 An example of a short-answer question from a practice English language exercise. In the top box, the teacher has given her feedback. The student's response is in the lower box

Source: English360 *Crossing Cultures* by Valentina Dodge

☑ Teacher feedback is provided in a timely fashion.

☑ Students can work through a practice exercise until they reach a correct or acceptable result.

Activity: Self-Assessment

Refer to Chapter 8 (see Figure 8.11 on page 167) for an example of an online self-assessment. Once students finish the self-assessment, they click on answers. A pop-up screen then appears with the answers.

Self-assessments should be used both to give students a sense of where they are in their course competencies and the pace they can use to progress.

 Go to the website for additional resources on practice activities.

Practice Exercise—Variation

Self-Assessment

Self-assessment activities have the following advantages in an online course. They:

- help students to pace their learning;
- serve as a tool for learner reflection;
- reinforce understandings because they are another form of built-in redundancy; and
- actively engage students in the course content and provide instantaneous feedback on their progress and knowledge.

 Self-correcting and/or self-assessment activities are used throughout the course to enable learners to vary the pace of their learning as is appropriate to the subject matter.

6.5 Group Projects

Types of Group Projects

There are many possibilities for group projects. We're highlighting two of the most common:

- an online presentation; and
- a research project/paper.

GROUP PROJECT

What?

At the most basic level, students can communicate online privately with their group members and share basic word processing, presentation, and spreadsheet documents. The advantage is that each group can have its work stored in one place.

Why?

Collaborative and group work is learner-centered. It requires that group members actively participate. They are responsible for their own learning and, in part, the learning of others.

Where?

Workgroups are designated spaces within the LMS that enable two or more students to collaborate and communicate. Each team has its own workgroup space, accessible exclusively to that team and the instructor. Teams cannot see each other's work; however, the teacher can see the work of all teams.

The workgroup tool varies significantly from one LMS to another. Some offer robust communication tools such as private group discussion forums, drop boxes for file storage and sharing, group wikis, and group email.

Who?

Groups.

How?

Organizing a group of students to work together on a project online requires the teacher to set up the necessary workspaces to facilitate the work, to have clear requirements for individual participation in the group, and to have expectations of where the final project is to be delivered (see also page 88, Types of Groups).

To set up a group project, the teacher needs to do the following:

1. Determine the team assignments. (*Note*: The teacher can only assign teams when the class begins.)
2. Create a workgroup space for each team.
3. Add the appropriate members to each team.
4. Notify the students of their team assignments via a course announcement and email them with clear instructions on how to access their team workgroup.

Activity: Online Group Presentation

There are many options for groups to make presentations. Presentations can be in the form of a prerecorded video, a slide presentation that is narrated, a simple slide presentation with notes, or a combination of text, images, audio, and video.

Group Project—Variation

Group Presentations

Table 6.1 shows a group project description for a team presentation. The students planned the presentation using communication and collaboration tools available to them within the workgroup.

Online group presentations have the following characteristics:

- Learners work together on a project and focus on communicating their findings in summary form.
- Presentations may include text, visuals, multimedia, and links to articulate products of the project work.

Activity: Group Research Project/Paper

When introducing new course material, consider having learners discover and experience it rather than simply read about it. Small research projects can help learners construct their own understandings of a subject through various self-selected resources.

The project becomes more meaningful because the learners, rather than the teacher, select the resources and topics. Learners are responsible for their own learning. In discussions with the class (peers and teacher), the sharing of multiple viewpoints and perspectives occurs naturally. The teacher is more engaged because even she does not know everything that will be presented. She may learn something new as well.

Table 6.2 An example of a group project/presentation

Group Project 3: Project Management and Industry Research

Learning outcomes

At the end of this project you will be able to:

- Develop a project plan with milestones, deliverables, and assigned tasks for this project using a project management collaborative tool, such as BaseCamp
- Critically compare and contrast collaboration technologies and the way they are used in a particular industry or sector
- Collaborate with an online team to develop a creative presentation

Description and Requirements

As a group, research the ways in which organizations in your assigned sector currently use technologies to collaborate in the workplace. Identify examples from reputable sources to support your presentation. These can include video, images, text, graphics, animations, diagrams, demonstrations, and charts. The group is encouraged to be creative with this presentation in terms of format and delivery.

Team industry/sector assignments:

- Team A—Research/Development
- Team B—Education
- Team C—Non-profits/Philanthropy Groups
- Team D—Information/Communication Technology
- Team E—Creative/Media

The presentation must include the following:

- Team name and names of all team members
- Each team member's role and responsibilities using a responsibility chart
- A description of the team's assigned sector
- The types of group collaborative activities within the sector
- The resources used in the research
- The ways in which the team conducted the research
- At least ten model examples of the ways in which specific organizations within the team's assigned sector use technology for the collaborative activities (as identified in item 4)

Grading Criteria and Percentage

All seven topics are appropriately covered		70 Points
• Clearly articulated and well-designed presentation This includes consistent font style, color scheme, layout, readability, and creativity		15 Points
• The project plan and project management tool was followed and utilized appropriately		10 Points
• Presentation met all submission requirements and rules and was submitted on time		5 Points
	Total	**100 Points**

Due Date

3/25, by 11:59 p.m. EST

Submission Location

Project 3 Drop Box Folder

Group Project—Variation

Team Research Project

Effective online team research projects have the following characteristics. They:

- situate students in an authentic context for conducting research using real tools and resources, such as online databases and library resources;
- guide students through the critical thinking process that moves students from novices toward being expert researchers; and
- allow the teacher and the groups to collaborate in the critique and assessment of research findings.

☑ There are sufficient opportunities for learners to work collaboratively.

☑ Learners are encouraged to interact with others (fellow classmates, course guests, etc.) and benefit from their experience and expertise.

☑ Procedures for group activities are specified so that students are aware of their role and responsibility in collaborative activities.

6.6 Summary and Standards

We introduced several types of activities that work well online. Refer to Table 6.3 (page 127) for a range of collaborative and individual activities. Many of these can also be used for class participation activities.

Now you have a basic understanding of a collection of activity environments that can be used for a wide range of involving and challenging learning experiences.

This collection offers many varied opportunities for learners to work collaboratively in groups. Learners are encouraged to interact with others (classmates, guests, the instructor, and outside resources), and benefit from others' experiences and expertise.

Table 6.3 Types of activities particularly suited to online courses

Activity Type	Activity Description
Problem-based learning	The activity presents a problem to be solved. The problem is genuine to the case or situation. The problem is presented within a realistic context. Learners have to actively apply their knowledge to solve the problem. The process is more important than the outcome (the answer). The problem may precede any lecture or presentation of new knowledge to the learner. It is the learner's role to determine what they need to learn to solve the problem.
Case study	Similar to problem-based learning, but presents a factually based complex problem in which there is not necessarily a right or wrong answer. The case is usually read individually and discussed as part of a larger group (class/team).
Project-based learning	The outcome is as important as the process. The outcome is typically a product (e.g. website, work of art, creative writing, science experiments, blueprints, etc.).
Simulations	Approximate a real-life experience with many variables in which the learner is situated in a role. The student has to make many decisions that affect the outcome of her role in the simulated environment.
Simulator-based activities	Provides learners with an opportunity to experience something that is near to impossible as a learner. This allows for failure without penalty (e.g. flying/crashing a plane, open-heart surgery). Simulators are used in the context of a larger activity, with goals, questions, etc.
Debates	A competitive activity that allows learners to apply their knowledge in the context of an argument. Usually done in teams.
Portfolio building	A collection of work amassed or collected over the duration of the course. This provides opportunities for learner reflection.
Critique	Engaging the students beyond whether they like or dislike something, with supporting evidence. Commonly used in art courses. This is great for critical thinking.
Primary research	An activity that involves gathering primary sources through interviews, questionnaires, and/or observation of events (e.g. research study).
Secondary research	An activity that involves reviewing secondary resources such as books, articles, etc. to create a literature review, annotated bibliography, etc.
Presentations	A demonstration of the learner's work summarized in a slide-show format, animation, video, audio, text, and/or a combination of these.
Practice exercises	A set of computer-graded questions (e.g. multiple choice, fill-in-the-blank, matching, true/false, etc.).
Receptive activities	Teacher audio/visual presentations and course readings. These are represented in course lessons as audio/video clips, pdf documents, and other presentation type formats such as PowerPoint and Google slide shows.

- [ ] Activities are frequent and varied. Students may respond to questions, select options, provide information, or interact with others.

- [ ] Activities engage students in higher-level thinking skills, including critical and creative thinking, analysis, and problem-solving.

- [ ] Course content is designed to encourage interactions between learners.

- [ ] Resources and activities support learning outcomes.

- [ ] Online spaces (e.g. discussion boards, social networks) are in place for students to participate in and meet outside the class.

- [ ] There are sufficient opportunities for learners to work collaboratively.

- [ ] Learners are encouraged to interact with others (fellow classmates, course guests, etc.) and benefit from their experience and expertise.

- [ ] Procedures for group activities are specified so that students are aware of their role and responsibility in collaborative activities.

- [ ] Teacher feedback is provided in a timely fashion.

- [ ] Students can work through a practice exercise until they reach a correct or acceptable result.

- [ ] Self-correcting and/or self-assessment activities are used throughout the course to enable learners to vary the pace of their learning as is appropriate to the subject matter.

Chapter 7 Resources that Engage

Now that you understand how a collection of activities works online (see Chapter 6), you can enhance them with multimedia resources and supplementary materials. In some cases, resources such as mini-video lectures, charts, images, and tables can be created by the teacher. In other cases, existing resources such as journal articles and links to websites are incorporated in the LMS. We discuss several types of resources in this chapter.

Resources break the monotony of teacher text or speaking when presenting new material. They add dimension to the learning experience. However, resources should not be used gratuitously. They may serve as embellishments to enhance student interest from time to time. But for the most part, they should be an integral part of the learning process and tasks for the lesson (see Scott Thornbury's presentation in Chapter 10 for an example of how this can work). All resources are directly related to the learning tasks.

Provide students with media-rich resources or guidance for finding their own resources to extend or amplify a course topic. This encourages students to go beyond the required materials and investigate on their own.

Resources can:

- illuminate the topic;
- add variety;
- introduce other viewpoints to encourage critical thinking;
- provide authentic, real-world examples;
- connect students with other voices in the real world;
- provide concrete examples; and
- support different learning styles.

Online resources covered in this chapter include the following:

- **text-based supplemental resources**—real-world writing accessible from online sources;

- **images**—photos, screenshots, charts, graphs, illustrations, etc.;

- **audio and video**;

- **voices and perspectives** from the world at large;

- **expert voices**—practitioners and academics;

- **experiences** from the field; and

- **websites and online Web-based tools**.

Learner-Centered Design

There has been a lot written on learner-centered design. Fundamentally, this model of teaching and learning requires learners to be active participants in their own learning. There are several elements that are needed for this type of design: activities, tools and resources, and social structures (Edelson & Reiser, 2006). Immersing learners in activities supports their active construction of knowledge.

Authenticity is also important. Work is made more meaningful to learners when it mirrors an authentic activity from the real world (e.g. students acting in the role of a manager who needs to schedule the staff to run a restaurant). Furthermore, learners (especially those in professional fields) need exposure to a community of experts and practitioners in the field to help them understand the culture in which the concepts and principles they are learning are applied in the real world.

 This chapter is supplemented by instructions on the website, on how to find and create resources.

7.1 Text-Based Supplemental Resources

In many fields, most supplemental resources are text-based. Well-chosen real-world texts support and enrich teacher-made and textbook content. Websites can provide a wealth of text materials in an authentic, contextualized format. Here are some examples of text-based resources:

- quotes, reviews, and critiques;

- newspapers and magazines;

Reprinted with permission

- historical speeches and documents;

- business documents, plans, letters, statistics, reports, and case studies;

- scientific studies, documents, and experiments;

- math problems, arguments, and examples; and

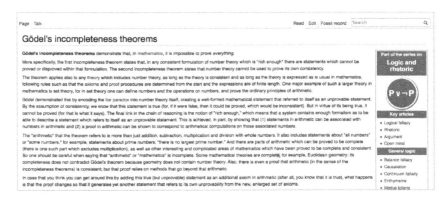

- international, political, and cultural documents and information.

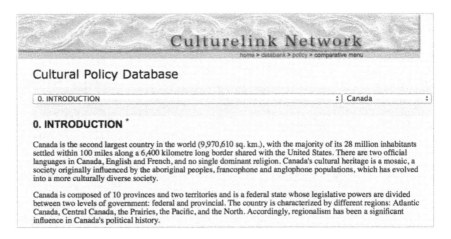

Many text-based materials are accessible through institutional online library services or the Internet. For example, ProQuest is a popular database of articles; most university libraries have subscriptions to this database. If something is assigned or recommended to students to retrieve, be sure they can all get to it. Provide direct links. Before the course is set to begin, check that all links are working. Also, check that the materials are up to date.

☑ **Correct, working links are provided to course materials and resources.**

Encourage students to find and contribute resources that further enhance the topic to promote a learning-centered approach. In some cases, they will find examples that are new to the teacher. Both the students and the teacher learn in such a situation.

☑ The consequences of plagiarism, cheating, and failure to properly cite copyrighted material are emphasized.

For guidance on how to find what you are looking for, many university and public libraries offer helpful orientation sessions, either live or online.

WEB For guidance on how to capture and embed text examples, refer to the website.

7.2 Images: Photos, Screenshots, Charts, Graphs, and Illustrations

note

Follow copyright law.

Many resources on the Internet can be used for educational purposes. If you do not see any information on whether the resources are free when you first enter a site, look for information under "terms of use" or a similar head in one of the site's menus. It is critical for the teacher and learner to ensure their use of resources is in line with the terms of use by the creators of the resources.

Embedding images, when appropriate and supportive of learning, is a first and fairly simple step in enhancing your online course. Some fields, such as art, science, and medicine, cannot really be taught without diagrams, illustrations, or photos. In others, such as literature, philosophy, and law, you may tend to use text exclusively. However, images can enhance and support the content, and when used appropriately in place of text can help learners process information in a meaningful way through the engagement of the visual sensory channel (Mayer, 2001). As we've said before, teaching online requires special strategies to vary the presentation of materials.

☑ Courses include a variety of relevant multimedia to support learning (e.g. audio, video, recommended podcasts, illustrations, photographs, charts, and graphs).

Refer to the typical LMS editing toolbar in Figure 7.1 to see the icons that you click on to enable you to embed links, images, and audio/video in your course. The common image formats accepted by most LMSs are JPEG, GIF, and PNG. Make sure your images are saved in one of these formats.

Figure 7.1 LMS editing toolbar

---

 to do

Flip through this book. Use it as a model.

This guide has many images, charts, and screenshots to help you work through the content. More, including audio and video segments, are available on the website.

What if this guide were written without this rich array of images and resources? How would this affect your understanding of the subject? Could we have communicated issues of online course design as effectively? If so, how? If not, why not?

Note also the care that was taken to make images clear and understandable (see Chapter 4).

What Kinds of Images Do You Need?

Scott Thornbury, a featured teacher (see page 85), created a linguistics course, Language Analysis for Teachers. Linguistics is certainly a text-based subject. Yet, you will see, when looking at his sample lesson (see page 194), that he uses images when helpful. Scott constantly varies the activities in his presentations to engage the students. He does this throughout the course when appropriate. None of the images are used gratuitously.

Scott needed to rethink the way he presents linguistics for an online environment. In the process, he enhances the subject matter and creates a learning environment that addresses a variety of learning styles.

When working with text-heavy subject matter, try to imagine how images might enhance your online presentation. With literature, for example, the visual arts, music, architecture, or design of the period may help students understand the content, philosophy, and style of what they are studying.

Where do you find images to use in your online course? For those of you who know what kind of images you are looking for, explore the many sites that are sure to be there in your field. There are many different search engines available that have different ways to search. Looking for images? In Google, you can do an "everything" search (see Figure 7.2). There, you can find a selection of resources on your topic and the websites where they appear. For example, Scott Thornbury has used images of chairs in one of his linguistics lessons (see page 196). He might have found them by using Google. His first search would bring up text references (see Figure 7.2). When the search results come up, Google gives you several options to refine the output, including **images**. See Figure 7.3 for an example of a refined image search.

note

Be conscious of copyright rules (see above).

Figure 7.2 An "everything" search in Google

WEB There is an easy way to search for openly licensed images on Google by going to Settings > Advanced Search. See the website for instructions.

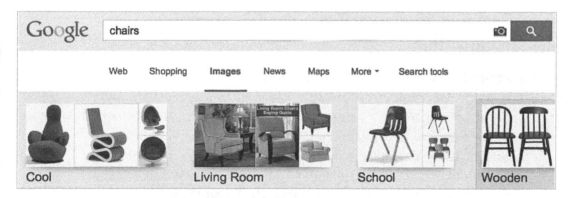

Figure 7.3 The "images" result set from Google

tip

Try using another search engine, such as Bing or Yahoo!, from time to time. You will notice that the search results can be very different. Use the one that suits you best.

Those of you who are not sure of what kind of images to use can search for inspiration and ideas. First, look at what others have done. How have people who deal with the same topics added dimension by using images on their websites?

Once you have some general ideas of what might work for you, move to the second stage and look for specific images for your topic. These can be photos, illustrations, charts, graphs, diagrams, or screenshots. All are searchable through Google Images.

For teachers who find they are teaching the same courses repeatedly, searching for and adding resources can broaden their perspective. This can be a refreshing and perhaps even inspiring activity for teachers.

For quantitative topics, create graphs, charts, and tables, when possible, to represent numerical information (see Figure 7.4). Pie charts, bar graphs, and line graphs are great ways to convey quantitative information to visual learners. It's critical that details such as the legend, axes, and labels of graphs and charts are readable, understandable, and clear.

Charts can also be a useful way to clarify concepts and organize information (see Figure 7.5).

- ☑ Details in images, graphs, charts, and diagrams are designed and organized so that they are easy to read and understand.

- ☑ Labeling in all presentation materials is accurate, readable, and clear.

Data Visualization

In the world of big data, almost every field has begun to create really interesting data visualizations. These visualizations can support students in identifying patterns or trends of massive data sets. Many of the visualizations are interactive and enable exploration of large data sets as well through a visual interface. Great examples can be found on the websites of the *New York Times*, the *Guardian*, the Gapminder Foundation, the World Bank, and many open-data websites such as NYC Open Data and City-Data.

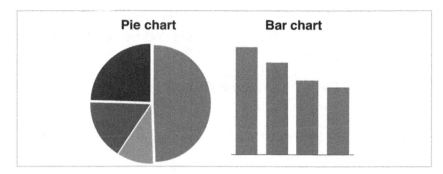

Figure 7.4 Examples of a basic pie and bar chart. Pie charts should be used to show proportions of a whole. Bar charts should be used for comparisons.

A funny thing	happened	on the way to the forum
NP	VP	PP
Subject (= the actor or agent)	Verb (= a process or state)	Adverbial (= circumstantial information, such as time, place or manner)

Figure 7.5 A chart created by Scott Thornbury to illustrate sentence elements

7.3   Audio and Video

Audio and video address specific learning styles. They can also add a personal feel, real-world experiences, dynamic examples, and dimension to the learning module. Mixing video or images with audible narration can also enhance learning by taking advantage of the fact that people can process information from both the auditory and visual channels when they do not conflict (e.g. **don't have voice narration while there is text on-screen**).

The Internet is a good source of video material, and published videos are often available with textbooks. Making your own is another option.

note
YouTube or Vimeo can be used for both audio and video.

Whether making audio and/or video clips is easy or even possible depends upon the equipment you have. Many computers come out-of-the box ready to make audio and video material, as do iPads, some tablets, and smartphones.

Most LMSs now include the ability to record video directly from your computer's webcam and microphone anywhere within the system.

 Refer to the website for suggestions on how to make your own materials.

 The format of media should be specified.

7.4 Varying Voices and Perspectives

Resources, whether teacher- or student-made, linked from the Web, or from guests to the class, give you the opportunity to bring other voices, opinions, and perspectives into the classroom. For example:

- Voices from the class—the teacher and students in various formats.

- Expert voices—practitioners and academics.

- Experiences from the field—workplace/worksite voices and situations.

The Teacher in Different Formats

One way to create textured presentation is by varying the way the teacher communicates with the class. When writing, for example, the teacher can alternate discussion board communications with blog postings and email as is appropriate. Embedded audio and video samples from the teacher provide relief from solidly textual communications.

Note: Scott Thornbury does this frequently in his courses. He sometimes uses video clips and sometimes audio (see page 197).

Such variations enable students to experience the teacher from different perspectives. It also models how the students may present themselves. Varying the way the teacher communicates can enhance content. Here are some examples:

- Audio and video commentary can introduce, summarize, or build in redundancy to clarify difficult concepts.

- Commentary may be the source of anecdotal information, examples, and tips.

- Teacher-made clips may reflect on a topic the teacher has asked the students to reflect on (see Figure 7.6).

- Clips may introduce an assignment or go over key factors after students have completed it.

Teachers can come up with good reasons to include such examples depending upon their style, priorities, and the content.

Keep audio and video segments short (around five minutes is a good length). This way, they read like a welcome break rather than another task. Watching long video clips can be tiresome. It's important to note that you are not replicating an on-site course lecture. Instead, you are creating a custom experience for the online student audience. For example, create a series of short videos for each topic. For a course in Operations Management, an introduction to the topic of *inventory management* was presented by the teacher. This was then followed by a problem–solution demonstration by the teacher in a second video. Then, in the third video concluding with a problem for the learners to solve based on the demonstration provided by the instructor (see Figure 7.6).

Recording lectures from an on-site course tends to be dry because it was intended for an on-site audience to experience in a live format. Even in an on-site format, long lectures supported by text-based slides are often dry and boring. The examples that follow show you how to design multimedia content appropriate for the online student audience.

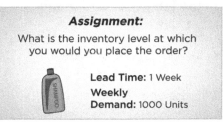

Figure 7.6
A teacher-created video sequence

Example 1: Narrated Support

In Figure 7.7, Scott Thornbury provides an audio explanation of a key concept in his linguistics course. Thinking of language in new ways requires some adjustment on the part of students. In this case, Scott is himself reflecting on a topic he has asked the students to reflect on. This also gives students another perspective on their teacher.

 You can see this audio in context on page 197 and listen to it on the website.

 Audio and video material appearing within a lesson should be brief.

Figure 7.7 An audio recording in Scott Thornbury's online class
Source: The New School/Matthew Sussman

The Students in Different Formats

Once the teacher has included some audio and video clips into the course, she can suggest that the students do the same in their presentations. Share the tools you learn about at the end of this chapter with the students as is appropriate. However, it is important to emphasize again that **the length of audio and video segments should be relatively brief**.

 Review and select some good examples of videos to share with the class or ask students to review videos and post their favorite, with an explanation as to why they have chosen it. Set clear criteria for them to reinforce their choices and focus their search. This type of activity engages the student and can be time-saving for the teacher.

Personal Perspective

Marjorie Vai

I once took a course on the history of graphic design. On the first day, the teacher gave each student the name of an important graphic designer. During the 12-week course, students would create and present an overview of the assigned designer and her work. This was narrated by the student.

I was struck by the simplicity and effectiveness of this activity. It is very important for graphic designers to present their own work effectively. So just doing this presentation was a learning activity that would serve students well in their careers.

All students viewed these presentations and learned from them and each student walked away with in-depth knowledge of a particular designer. It was an engaging and satisfying experience for all.

 to do

Expert Voices—Practitioners and Academics

We have included our voices and the voices of practitioners in this book. Has this made the guidelines and explanations seem more authentic? Has this enhanced the knowledge presented in the book? How? Why? Jot down some notes on this and think about how and why a similar approach might benefit students.

Example 1: Direct Expert Interaction

A guest speaker, whether a practitioner or an academic, brings another voice and a source of expertise into the online class. In a direct interaction, the guest speaker communicates directly with the students in some way. The guest should first be introduced to the students. Here are some examples:

- a reading assignment related to the guest;

- a summary biography and/or an example of the guest's work;

- a research assignment on some aspect of the guest's work, company, or institution;

- an audio or video clip of the guest in performance or being interviewed; and

- an audio clip, slide show, or video clip of a series of the guest's works.

How the guest is presented to the students will depend upon the nature of the guest's work and how this relates to what is being studied.

Next, the guest interacts with the students. Here are some examples:

- The teacher creates a discussion forum for the class to interact with one another over a few days or a week. The guest visits over this period of time and responds to students' posts.

- The guest joins a live (synchronous) class session via video conference.

- The guest visits a project website and then comments or critiques it via audio, video, or in group discussion forums.

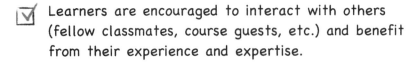 **Learners are encouraged to interact with others (fellow classmates, course guests, etc.) and benefit from their experience and expertise.**

Example 2: Indirect Expert Interaction

In an indirect expert interaction, the students respond to the expert in some way, and the teacher comments and communicates with the students.

Figure 7.8 is an example that provides the students with another form of real-life input into the course. The students respond to the guest's blog posts and the teacher provides feedback on the students' posts.

note

The activity was modified for the purposes of this book.

This example is from Professor Lehrer's course on Advanced Business Writing taught at NYU.

Activity: PowerPoint Blog

Hi All: We have a guest writer for this week's blog— Lucy Rivers. She has written a blog about using PowerPoint to effectively deliver compelling presentations. The blog has been posted in our online course, and can be found by clicking on blogs.

Please respond to her thoughts with your own by next Monday, February 8th. Make sure to use an outline to organize your thoughts, and compose your response off line so that you can proof it properly.
If you have any questions, please post them in the Q&A discussion forum.

Thanks

Professor Lehrer

Figure 7.8 An activity that brings in expert commentary

Example 3: Expert Audio and Video Clips (from the Internet)

It is fairly easy to find online mini-lectures that are freely available on the Internet in all subject areas. At the writing of this book, one very prominent example is the Khan Academy (see Figure 7.9). The narrator explains the concepts while speaking and writing on the digital blackboard that is recorded as a video.

The goal of the Khan Academy is to use technology to provide a free, world-class education to anyone, anywhere. See more information about this site at: www.khanacademy.org/about.

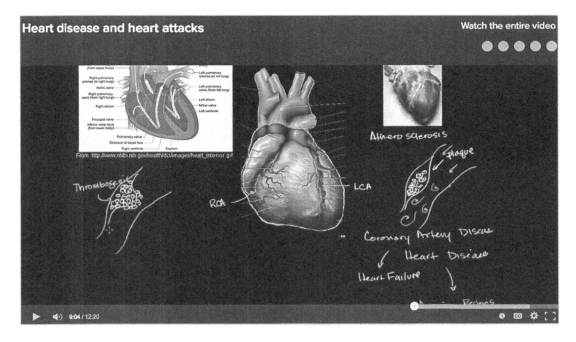

Figure 7.9 Khan Academy: A presentation on the relationship of heart disease to heart attacks (reprinted with permission)

The Flipped Classroom

The flipped classroom is a teaching approach in which homework and lectures are reversed. That is, in face-to-face classes, class time is spent working on problems, discussions, and group activities. The foundational concepts, theories, and introduction of new knowledge happen online.

Traditional in-class lectures may be replaced with short online lectures. The ease in producing short video lectures and multimedia tutorials has made this approach to on-site teaching very popular. This approach is natural for a blended learning class.

iences from the Field

al study areas such as medicine, social work, and "field" refers to the term "fieldwork." Resources from rovide real-life exposure to users, clients, patients, customers, and situations related to the class's area of study. The subjects are the kinds of people or situations that the students might encounter or engage with when they eventually work in their area of expertise. For academic subjects such as languages, literature, and research, "field" refers to the subject area. Guests may include researchers, graduate students, writers, etc.

Audio

How important is language knowledge?

Listen to these five people responding to that question. Which of them best represents your own position?:

The first two are **experienced teachers**;

1   2

the third is a **relatively inexperienced teacher**;

3

the fourth is an advanced, Spanish-speaking, **student of English**;

4

and the fifth is a **teacher trainer**.

5

Figure 7.10 Audio activity from Scott Thornbury's class

Voices from the field serve as a means of bringing the voices and perspectives of different players into the class. Their perspectives may be cultural, educational, economic, social, or political. Be sure that the materials represent current issues. Furthermore, through exposure to professionals in the field, learners can "learn (and practice) professional discourse" (Quintana et al., 2006, p. 123).

This is an excellent way to expose students to the realities they will face and give them a real feel for the subject matter in a chosen field, occupation, or profession. Even if the field does not represent their primary area of study, such exposure enriches the learning experience.

In a practical field, this may also be a way to bring in current issues related to best practices. These could vary from discussions of how to do research, teach, create something, or set up a good interview, to the tone and content of doctor/patient, or teacher/student, or customer services manager/representative exchanges.

Example: Input from the Field

Scott Thornbury created audio recordings of a variety of players in the language teaching and learning field. Each comment is very short and to the point (see Figure 7.10).

☑ Teacher, peer-to-peer, guest, and automated feedback clarifies, amplifies, and extends the topic.

☑ Topics and materials are up to date and relevant.

☑ Materials are authentic or relate to real-life applications.

☑ Presentations, activities, and assessments address a variety of learning abilities and preferences.

7.6 Web-Based Tools

Web-based apps and software are core components when developing resources. In general, most audio and video production can take place on your laptop using your webcamera and microphone. Software applications include: iMovie and VSDC Free Video Editor; also, for screencasting software, look at Captivate or Screenflow. Other options include mobile apps that you can use on your tablet to produce multimedia presentations and publish them to the Web. Also, the latest LMSs have built-in tools to create short video recordings and screencasts. Teachers are in the best position to determine what would add value to their content.

WEB **On the website, we introduce a series of tools with short descriptions and links. In most cases, we will provide links to tutorials and/or details on how to use the tool.**

7.7 Accessibility

We end this chapter with a final but very important point. Careful attention must be paid to ease of accessibility of resources. We emphasize especially these four points:

*   **Format.** Whatever the resources, they must be made available to students in a format that they can access. For example, if you know that class videos will require special software such as QuickTime, students should be informed early on in the course so they can ensure they have the right software installed.

- **Links.** Cross-referencing is another area of accessibility that is critical. If a resource is not right there where it is referred to, it should be available by clicking on a link. The clickable link itself should describe what it is linking to rather than being a URL (e.g. Google rather than www.google.com).

- **Portability.** Whether you're using an LMS or your own website, test it out on a mobile device such as a phone or tablet. Also, large text documents, video, and audio should be available for download when possible so that students can access and review them on the go.

- **Assistive technologies.** Making resources accessible goes beyond making them easy to use. Learners with vision impairments rely on various assistive products to access computer-based information, such as screen readers, which translate what's on a computer screen into automated audible output, and refreshable Braille displays. In the US, the standards for this type of accessibility can be found at: www.section508.gov. We recommend that you check with your institution on compliance regulations relating to the use of assistive technologies.

☑ Resource material is accessible to all students in commonly used formats.

☑ Cross-referencing and links to items in other parts of the course are provided.

☑ Course material is portable (e.g. text can be downloaded or printed out, material is well designed for handheld devices).

Finally, this standard speaks for itself:

☑ Bibliographies and reference lists include a variety of resources, including Web links, books, journals, video, and downloadable text and audio files as is appropriate.

7.8 Summary and Standards

This chapter has provided you with ways to include supplemental text, images, audio and video recordings, and Web-based tools into your online course. Refer to Chapters 6 and 10 when thinking about incorporating resources for online presentations and activities.

- [ ] Resource material is accessible to all students in commonly used formats.

- [ ] Courses include a variety of relevant multimedia to support learning (e.g. audio, video, recommended podcasts, illustrations, photographs, charts, and graphs).

- [ ] The consequences of plagiarism, cheating, and failure to properly cite copyrighted material are emphasized.

- [ ] Details in images, graphs, charts, and diagrams are designed and organized so that they are easy to read and understand.

- [ ] Labeling in all presentation materials is accurate, readable, and clear.

- [ ] The format of media should be specified.

- [ ] Audio and video material appearing within a lesson should be brief.

- [ ] Learners are encouraged to interact with others (fellow classmates, course guests, etc.) and benefit from their experience and expertise.

- [ ] Teacher, peer-to-peer, guest, and automated feedback clarifies, amplifies, and extends the topic.

- [ ] Topics and materials are up to date and relevant.

- [ ] Materials are authentic or relate to real-life applications.

- [ ] Presentations, activities, and assessments address a variety of learning abilities and preferences.

☐ Cross-referencing and links to items in other parts of the course are provided.

☐ Course material is portable (e.g. text can be downloaded or printed out, material is well designed for handheld devices).

☐ Correct, working links are provided to course materials and resources.

☐ Bibliographies and reference lists include a variety of resources, including Web links, books, journals, video, and downloadable text and audio files as is appropriate.

Chapter 8 | Assessment and Feedback

This chapter covers the important elements of assessment and feedback, with specific considerations for online courses. In the course design process, it is critical to plan how you will assess students, create the assessments, and communicate to students where and how they will be assessed. Also, planning the timing and form of the feedback on those assessments will help you organize your time when teaching the course. The key elements covered in this chapter are:

- assessment and learning outcomes;

- variety and timing of assessments;

- teacher feedback;

- self-assessment;

- peer-to-peer feedback;

- learner expectations and requirements; and

- grading criteria.

8.1 Assessing Learning Outcomes

Keep in mind that **assessment is clearly and directly tied to the learning outcomes of the course**. Performance is measured through the products of the learner's work. Products may include papers, assignments, tests, quizzes, digital presentations, and projects.

As we described in Chapter 5, class participation takes the form of activities that engage the online learner. The quality and quantity of interactions among all parties (including course guests) is key to the success of learning—especially in an online course. To signal its importance, **class participation is graded**, as a percentage of the final grade.

Refer to Figure 8.1. This is the introduction to the first week of Kristen Sosulski's Collaboration Technologies online course at NYU. It includes specific outcomes for a week online. Note that the wording is clear and definite. The terms **name**, **identify**, **describe**, **apply**, and **categorize** clearly indicate what students need to demonstrate. These terms are also **measurable**, and can relate to a range of thinking skills.

Introduction

Welcome to Collaboration Technologies!

This is a great course to take online since all the technologies that we'll be reviewing and using are Web-based. This course is offered in an intensive 6-week format. It's important that you keep up with the course readings and honor the due dates for assignments and activities.

In this course we will explore possibilities afforded by and through various communication and collaborative technologies. Please review the syllabus carefully. The syllabus will provide you with an overview of the course content areas, requirements, required readings, and outline of assignments.

The bulk of the course content is available in the **Lessons** area of the course website. It includes all of the readings, course content, and assignments that are required from **Monday, June 28 through Sunday, July 4**.

A major goal for this first week is for you to become oriented with the learning management system (LMS) in which you will be studying, communicating, and submitting your course assignments.

By the end of this lesson **you will be able to**:

- **describe** the importance of the collaborative process and factors that influence and shape the participants' contributions in collaborative workspaces;
- **define and categorize** the six types of e-collaboration technologies;
- **apply** the electronic collaboration framework to your own academic and professional experience using collaborative technologies; and
- **identify** and **categorize** new e-collaboration technologies, and **reflect**, **describe**, and **share** your experiences using two types of e-collaboration tools.

Figure 8.1 Collaboration Technologies, Week 1, lesson introduction

Refer to Figure 8.2 for an example of a **class participation activity** from Kristen's course that is designed to measure student achievement of the learning outcomes. This is a two-part activity. This example demonstrates the relationship between learning outcomes (what students are expected to be able to do) and how those outcomes are being assessed. Note the specifics on grading, due dates and times, and location within the LMS where the students should go to complete the assignment. Communicating these details to students makes the teacher's goals explicit and directs the students appropriately.

Class Participation Assignment

Part 1

After completing the ice-breaker activities and the readings for week 1, respond to the following here in the discussion forum:

Reflect on your own experience using collaborative technologies. Specifically, provide two examples of e-collaboration technologies that you have used in the past. Do the following:

1. Name the e-collaborative technology.
2. Describe the collaborative task.
3. Describe the participants in the collaborative task.
4. Describe the physical environment of the participants.
5. Describe the social environment of the participants.

Due—7/2, 11:59 p.m. EST

Part 2

Next, between 7/2 and 7/4 respond to your assigned partner's posting by categorizing the technology that they described. Provide two other examples of technologies that fall into the same category.

Due—7/4, 11:59 p.m. EST

Figure 8.2 Collaboration Technologies, Week 1, topical discussion activity

☑ The relationship between learning outcomes and assessments is evident.

☑ Assessments determine the degree to which the learners have achieved the required learning outcomes.

☑ Activities lead to active interactions that involve course content and personal communication.

8.2 Ongoing and Varied Assessment

Rather than using just one method, robust assessment requires the critical analysis of multiple forms of evidence that learning outcomes have been attained.

(Reeves, 2006, p. 304)

Assess online students on an ongoing basis. This gives them multiple opportunities to improve upon and reinforce their knowledge and skills. Assessing online learners regularly highlights where the students are in their learning process.

Ongoing assessment provides:

* quantifiable evidence of learner engagement and participation;

* opportunities to give feedback to learners;

* demonstrable measures of learner progress within the course; and

* an opportunity for learners to test and apply their knowledge and skills.

It is also important to evaluate learner performance based on a variety of assessment types (i.e. not just tests). **Not all skills and knowledge can be evaluated with the same measurement technique.** Varied types of activities are encouraged and are easy to design for online once you know the basics. These can include online class discussions and group projects. This also builds in a safeguard against cheating. When you have multiple assessments in different forms, you can better gauge students' performance.

Course includes ongoing and frequent assessment.

 Graded assignments are varied (e.g. special projects, reflective assignments, research papers, case studies, presentations, group work, etc.).

8.3 Teacher Feedback

Good teacher feedback on assessments promotes and improves learning. Specifically, the role of feedback is to:

- expand upon the learner's knowledge;

- help the learner understand how to improve and progress within the course;

- address misconceptions and misunderstandings, and correct mistakes; and

- motivate learners by promoting a positive attitude toward the challenges of the activity and their progress in it.

Ongoing assessment engages the learner throughout the course. This is especially true when teacher feedback is timely. Regular and timely feedback helps students to improve. It should highlight areas that need improvement, present suggestions for future learning, and indicate where progress has been made.

It is important that you communicate when and how students will receive feedback on their work. In an on-site course, the teacher may announce this in class. In an online class, the teacher can **use the announcements tool to communicate to learners when and how feedback is given on a particular assignment**. Refer back to Chapter 3 to review writing announcements.

 Teacher feedback is provided in a timely fashion.

8.4 Other Types of Feedback

As previously discussed, feedback from the teacher should be continual, with regular opportunities for assessment of the learner's work. Feedback can also come from peers and class guests who have expertise in the course's content. And keep in mind that **self-assessment is an excellent reflective tool**. Refer to the Assessment and Feedback Plan in Table 8.1 to see how other types of feedback are provided to learners in an online course. The plan clearly indicates who is to give feedback and when.

Peer-to-Peer Feedback

When learners receive feedback on their work from their peers:

- Learners feel that the products of their work are not only relevant to the teacher, but that a larger audience is evaluating and commenting on their work and may benefit from the experience.

- Learners develop the skills to critically assess the work of others.

- Assessing the work of others may lead to self-reflection in approaching their own work.

- Multiple perspectives on the same topic may lead to richer understandings and synthesis.

When requiring students to provide feedback to others on their work, set up the criteria for evaluation. This is critical for group projects, where each member evaluates another's contributions.

Guest Feedback

Feedback from guests, such as experts in the field, can tie the activity to a real-world context for the learner. In an online course, it is easy to involve guests from anywhere in the world. Involve experts in the feedback process. They can serve as reviewers of learner work such as group presentations or papers.

Feedback Form
Group 1

1. Describe the most important outcome, finding, or idea presented by the group today?

2. How well did the group do at selecting an interesting story to tell with the data as it related to their topic and audience?

Poor   Neutral   Excellent

1   2   3   4   5   6   7

3. Which of the four visualizations did you find particularly compelling? Explain.

4. In your opinion, how well did students do at selecting visual displays (chart types) to present their data? For example, were they appropriate and easy to read and interpret?

Poor   Neutral   Excellent

Figure 8.3 A feedback form created for experts to comment on aspects of student work

See Figure 8.3 for an example of a feedback form designed by the teacher to solicit feedback from experts on student projects.

Teacher and Automatic Computer-Generated Feedback

Most LMSs are equipped with a tool to design online self-tests, quizzes, or exams with instantaneous feedback. See "Practice Exercises" in Chapter 6 for examples of such question types available in the test/quizzes tool.

The feedback for tests and quizzes is less involved than it is in practice exercises. There, because we are using these exercises as a learning tool, we are enabling students to keep working on the exercises until they get to the right answer.

Use teacher, peer-to-peer, guest, and automated feedback to clarify, amplify, and extend a topic.

Keep in mind that **automatic feedback is especially good for periodic self-assessments** (see Chapter 6).

☑ Teacher, peer-to-peer, guest, and automated feedback clarifies, amplifies, and extends the topic.

☑ Criteria and procedures for peer review and evaluation are clear.

☑ Self-correcting and/or self-assessment activities are used throughout the course to enable learners to vary the pace of their learning as is appropriate to the subject matter.

Ways to Provide Feedback in an Online Course

Feedback can be automated for multiple-choice tests, quizzes, and practice exercises in the LMS. This feedback can be given instantaneously or after learners complete the assessment. The feedback may be a sentence or two written by the teacher for both correct and incorrect answers.

note

The feedback is immediate. This is one of the benefits of an online course.

For student work produced in word processing programs (i.e. essays, research papers) such as Microsoft Word or Pages, feedback can be provided directly in the document itself using "comments." The comments are linked to the specific words, sentences, or paragraphs (see Figure 8.4). The annotated papers can then be returned to students (via email or through the LMS) with the feedback embedded.

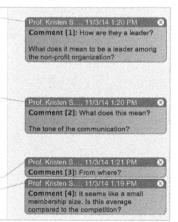

When compared to their direct competition, The Organization is a leader among the non-profit architecture organizations. However all such organizations have similar issues with a lack of a large online community. Most of their communities are comprised of social media spectators with little to no conversation occurring outside of their managed communities.

Prof. Kristen S..., 11/3/14 1:20 PM
Comment [1]: How are they a leader?
What does it mean to be a leader among the non-profit organization?

In order to grow The Organization's online presence with the end result being an increase in donations, we recommend that they focus on building their online community through tools and modification of online tone. We will look to other related online audiences to increase followership.

Prof. Kristen S..., 11/3/14 1:20 PM
Comment [2]: What does this mean?
The tone of the communication?

PART 1: Initial Analysis - A Snapshot. Establishing a baseline

The Organization maintains a website, through which it collects newsletter subscribers and new members, among other things. Based on recent Google analytics stats, the website gets approximately 334k page views annually. The newsletter email list has 14,000 subscribers and The Organization has approximately 300+ paying members. As far as community types are concerned, The Organization does not have a directly managed community, but it does have several managed communities and a few participating communities. Managed communities

Prof. Kristen S..., 11/3/14 1:21 PM
Comment [3]: From where?
Prof. Kristen S..., 11/3/14 1:19 PM
Comment [4]: It seems like a small membership size. Is this average compared to the competition?

Figure 8.4 Teacher feedback on a student essay in Microsoft Word

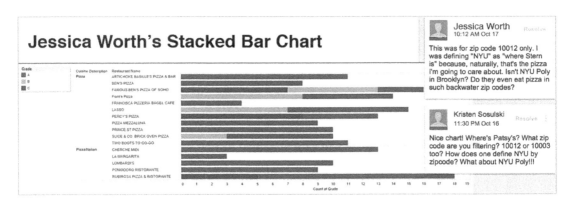

Figure 8.5 Teacher feedback on a chart designed by a learner using Google Docs

Also, Google Docs is a popular way to share and edit documents on the Web. Teachers and students can provide comments on Google Docs online. This enables multiple people to comment on a single document (see Figure 8.5).

Table 8.1 presents a partial Assessment and Feedback Plan for a six-week course. This is a tool that teachers can use to assist in their planning about when and how feedback is given. Each activity type is mapped to a given week within the course and a corresponding grade percentage.

There are three visible points of engagement for each week of the course. In this example, there are ungraded activities (Practice Exercises) and graded activities (Class Discussions, an Online Journaling Activity, and a Group Project). **Teacher and peer-to-peer feedback is regular.** In addition, the Group Project presents an opportunity for feedback from the teacher, peers, and a class guest.

Drafting an Assessment and Feedback Plan is an essential tool for the teacher in planning an online course. It serves as a reminder of when grading and feedback are required when the course is in progress. It also outlines the stages of learner and teacher engagement throughout the duration of the course.

 To begin designing your plan, refer to Table 8.1 and use the online template. Think about the following:

- What are the key assignments, quizzes, and activities?

- Which activities are graded and which ones are not?

- Who will be giving feedback and when?

Table 8.1 An Assessment and Feedback Plan for the first two weeks of an online course

Assessment and Feedback Plan				
Week #	Learner Activities	% of Grade	Feedback Given By	Feedback Turnaround
1	Practice Exercise	0	Automated	Immediately
	Class Discussion	5	Teacher, Peers	Throughout the week's discussion
	Online Journal	5	Teacher	Within a week
2	Practice Exercise	0	Automated	Immediately
	Class Discussion	5	Teacher, Peers	Throughout the week's discussion
	Group Project	10	Teacher, Peers, Guest	Within a week

☑ Students know when and how they will receive feedback from instructors.

☑ Graded elements are clearly distinguished from those that are ungraded.

☑ The relationship between graded elements and the final grade is clear.

8.5 Setting Learner Expectations

The following is a list of clear grading criteria that clarifies learner expectations for each assessment:

• Each graded item is explained clearly in the syllabus accompanied by a percentage designation and in the corresponding assignments or activities.

• The grading criteria detail how each item's score correlates to the specific requirements for each assignment or activity (this can be done using a rubric).

note

This approach is not uniform across all LMSs.

- For ungraded items, it is still important to specify expectations in order to make learners aware of the criteria for excellent performance and/or work.

- The graded items are recorded in the online grade book.

The online grade book allows learners to track their progress within the course and check immediately when a grade has been assigned. See Figure 8.6 for a view of a single student's progress as noted in the online grade book.

Name	Due	Score	Out of	
Participation 1	Aug 25 by 11:59pm	4.75	5	✓
Participation 2	Sep 29 by 11:59pm	5	5	✓
Participation 3	Oct 27 by 11:59pm	5	5	✓
Project 1	Nov 21 by 11:59pm	94	100	✓
Participation 4	Nov 24 by 11:59pm	5	5	✓
Participation 5	Dec 29 by 11:59pm	3	5	✓
Participation		**91%**		25% of Final
Projects		**94%**		75% of Final
Total		**93.3%**		

Figure 8.6 A view of a single student's progress in the online grade book from the teacher's perspective

note

The specific requirements for individual assignments are not outlined in the syllabus, but rather in the assignments section of your online course (see Figure 8.7).

The following items must be communicated to the learner for each online assignment and activity:

- activity title;

- instructions and requirements;

- grading criteria;

- due date;

- location for submission (discussion forum, assignment upload, drop box, blog); and

- where and when the learner will receive teacher feedback.

Assignment 2

Due Dec 22 by 11:59pm   **Points** 10

Complete the assignment below. Submit your work as a single document to NYU Classes > Data Visualization > Assignments > Assignment 2. The document must contain the following:

- Your name
- Part 1 - Embed screenshots of your 3 charts in a Word document. For each visualization, include the audience, task, data, and display selected.
- Part 2 - Optional - Include a screenshot of your visualization
- Part 3 - Optional - Include the solutions to the exercises provided.

PART 1: Applying the data visualization process

Data:	Download players.csv from NYU Classes > Data Visualization > Resources or from http://bit.ly/playerscsv ⌐ .
Tool(s):	Tableau Desktop
	Create three visualizations based on the players.csv data using Tableau. This data set represents the total dollars played by player and game for Station Casinos in Las Vegas over a 24 hour time period. There are seven game types: Slots, Blackjack (BJ), Craps, Baccarat (Bac), Bingo, Poker, and Other.
Task:	The first chart should answer the following questions: What is the ranking of seven games with respect total revenue to the casino? How well did each game perform? What is the highest performer? Lowest?
	The second and third charts are open ended. Your goal is to work with the data set to visualize other interesting attributes of the data set. Be sure to label and describe your charts appropriately in Tableau.
Submission:	Embed the PDFs of your three charts (or you can use screenshots). For each visualization, describe the audience, task, data, and display selected.

Figure 8.7 An assignment described to students in the assignments section of the LMS

If you are using an LMS's assignment feature, it will prompt you to enter many of these elements, such as title, grading scheme, due date, and submission type.

☑ Grading criteria are outlined in the course syllabus and within the assignment or assessment itself.

☑ Students are given clear expectations and criteria for assignments. Examples are included for clarification when needed.

☑ Students can easily track their progress.

8.6 Assessment of Activities

Table 8.2 presents the general **productive** and **reflective** activity types covered in Chapter 6 and corresponding assessment strategies. Examples of assessment measurements

Table 8.2 General assessments for different activity types

Activity	Assessment Strategy
Class Discussions and Class Participation	A class participation **rubric** is completed by students as a check to ensure they have fulfilled the criteria. Student participation is evaluated by the teacher using the rubric and the specific activity requirements.
Online Journaling	Student self-assessment and informal teacher feedback.
Shared Knowledge Base	Teacher assesses the contributions of each individual and/or group.
Practice Exercises (sometimes self-assessment)	Teacher assesses exercises for participation, rather than for correctness or incorrectness. Student assesses his own progress based on teacher or automatic computer-generated feedback.
Group Projects	Teacher assesses the group project as a whole. Team members complete a peer assessment. Teacher reviews peer assessment and factors in the student's individual grade for the group project. Each student's role in the group is clear.

are provided for class participation and peer-to-peer evaluation of group projects.

Class Discussion and Class Participation

Class participation in an online course is a critical support for online engagement. Assessing learner engagement throughout the online course motivates and guides the learner.

All **learners must actively contribute to class discussions**. This requires posting regularly to the forum, at least two or three times per week. Setting up small weekly class participation activities supports active participation.

Classroom participation in an online course often takes place in the **discussion forum**. Online class participation should account for between 10 percent and 30 percent of the course grade. Active participation in discussions cultivates community within a course. It also provides the teacher with a clear indication of each learner's level of engagement.

Table 8.3 An example of a class participation rubric (from Kristen's course) used to assess student postings in the discussion forum

Evaluation Criteria	Does not meet any of the requirements	Partially meets the requirements	Most meets requirements	Meets all requirements	Exceeds requirements
Quality	Contributions to the online class discussion are well written, proofread, and directly relevant to the discussion topic.				
	0	1–2	3	4	5
Accuracy	All contributions are supported with evidence, if required. Sharing personal experiences is essential to this course, however applying and referencing the salient course readings, cases, and other literature is critical.				
	0	1–2	3	4	5
Timeliness	Contributions were made within the assigned time period.				
	0	1–2	3	4	5

Rubric

A rubric is a tool that "defines the performance levels for each gradable activity element."

(Conrad & Donaldson, 2004, p. 26).

In the **syllabus**, specify the course expectations for participation. To foster participation, the requirements are clearly outlined and class participation counts toward the final grade. The rubric in Table 8.3 illustrates how the grading for class participation can be defined. The rubric in Figure 8.8 describes the level of performance expected for levels of quality, accuracy, and timeliness. Specifically, "rubrics help the student figure out how their project[s], [assignments, activities, and participation] will be evaluated" (ALTEC, 2008, para 1).

Teacher feedback is provided to students through comments in the discussion forum. The teacher also provides a grade for each activity in the grade book (see Figure 8.9). Most LMSs have a grade book. This is another form of feedback for those graded activities. In this example, each class participation activity is worth 5 percent of the grade. Each activity is assessed based on three criteria (quality, accuracy, and timeliness) on a 0 to 5 point scale.

This concrete approach clarifies the relationship between class participation and the course grade. It also advises learners that participation is assessed throughout the course.

Participation Rubric

Criteria	Ratings						Pts
Quality: Contributions to the online class discussion are well written, proofread, and directly relevant to the discussion topic	Exceeds Requirements 5 pts	All Met 4 pts	Mostly Met 3 pts	Somewhat Met 2 pts	Barely Met 1 pts	Not Met 0 pts	5 pts
Accuracy: All contributions are supported with evidence, if required. Sharing personal experiences is essential to this course; however, applying and referencing the salient course readings, cases, and other literature is critical.	Exceeds Requirements 5 pts	All Met 4 pts	Mostly Met 3 pts	Somewhat Met 2 pts	Barely Met 1 pts	Not Met 0 pts	5 pts
Timeliness: Contributions are made within the assigned time period.	Exceeds Requirements 5 pts	All Met 4 pts	Mostly Met 3 pts	Somewhat Met 2 pts	Barely Met 1 pts	Not Met 0 pts	5 pts
						Total Points: 15	

Figure 8.8 An example of a class participation rubric (from Kristen Sosulski's course) used to assess student postings in the discussion forum

Student Name	Participation 1 Out of 5	Participation 2 Out of 5	Participation 3 Out of 5	Participation 4 Out of 5	Participation 5 Out of 5
Betty McGonigal	4.75	5	5	5	3

Figure 8.9 An example of class participation grades as noted in the online grade book within the LMS

☑ Class participation/discussion should account for 10–30 percent of the final grade.

☑ Criteria/rubrics clearly inform learners as to how they will be assessed on specific assignments, such as online class participation.

to do

Think about how you plan to assess class participation

Conducting a discussion in an online forum is one of many ways to engage students in a dialogue in an online class. If you require the students to participate in an online asynchronous discussion for a specified time period, you need to state this clearly.

Think about your online class. Respond to the following questions:

- How many posts per week will be required?
- How will the quality of each post be measured?
- Will the time between posts be important?
- What does a post consist of: words, audio, video, and/or slide shows?
- Is length or number of items a factor?

tip

Some LMSs come equipped with survey tools to help you develop these peer assessment forms. An alternative is to use free online tools such as Survey Monkey or Google Forms to create an online peer evaluation form, and send the link to the students. You can then view the results online. You can also include an option for students to either put their name on the form or keep it anonymous.

Group Projects

Group projects require teacher and peer-to-peer assessment. The best-designed team projects include **team** and **individual assessment** by the teacher (Educause, 2010) in addition to **peer-to-peer assessment**.

The assessment of **individual student performance** in a group project can be tricky. Be sure to delineate or have the team assign roles to each member. The roles and responsibilities of each student in the team should be clear.

The teacher can structure the peer-to-peer assessment by providing a peer assessment form (see Figure 8.10). The peer assessment form measures the participation of all team members. Students rate each team member according to a prescribed set of criteria. These forms can be designed for students to complete at the end of a group project, or periodically throughout the project work.

Personal Perspective

Kristen Sosulski

I take a democratic approach to teamwork. In my online courses, when I assign a group project, I require that the team identify a project manager/leader who will take minutes on all the group meetings that include roles, responsibilities, key action items, and next steps with due dates. This helps me assess the work of individuals within a team. I then review the peer-to-peer assessments of each team member by the team. This gives me a clear understanding of who did what.

Group Project Peer Evaluation Form - Level of Participation - Project #2: Group A					✎ 🔍 🗑
Criteria	**Ratings**				**Pts**
Kelly Brown, Project Manager	Went beyond the assigned deliverables. Regularly volunteered for additional roles and tasks. 4 pts	Always active. Completed the assigned deliverables based on his/her role. Contributions were of value to the group. 3 pts	Usually active. Marginal contributions to deliverables, but contributions were of value to the group. 2 pts	Minimal. Contributions to group deliverables were incomplete or incorrect. 1 pts	None. 0 pts	4 pts
James Dixon, Researcher	Went beyond the assigned deliverables. Regularly volunteered for additional roles and tasks. 4 pts	Always active. Completed the assigned deliverables based on his/her role. Contributions were of value to the group. 3 pts	Usually active. Marginal contributions to deliverables, but contributions were of value to the group. 2 pts	Minimal. Contributions to group deliverables were incomplete or incorrect. 1 pts	None. 0 pts	4 pts
Yelena Jones, Writer	Went beyond the assigned deliverables. Regularly volunteered for additional roles and tasks. 4 pts	Always active. Completed the assigned deliverables based on his/her role. Contributions were of value to the group. 3 pts	Usually active. Marginal contributions to deliverables, but contributions were of value to the group. 2 pts	Minimal. Contributions to group deliverables were incomplete or incorrect. 1 pts	None. 0 pts	4 pts
Joseph Zu, Presenter	Went beyond the assigned deliverables. Regularly volunteered for additional roles and tasks. 4 pts	Always active. Completed the assigned deliverables based on his/her role. Contributions were of value to the group. 3 pts	Usually active. Marginal contributions to deliverables, but contributions were of value to the group. 2 pts	Minimal. Contributions to group deliverables were incomplete or incorrect. 1 pts	None. 0 pts	4 pts
					Total Points: 16

Figure 8.10 A simple peer assessment form for assessing member participation in group projects

 Another example of a peer assessment form can be found on the website. It provides a way for each member of the group to assign a grade percentage for each team member. The grades for all team members must equal 100 percent.

For teacher assessment and feedback on team projects considering developing a group project assessment rubric, see the website.

Self-Assessment

Incorporating self-assessment and reflective activities helps students recognize where they are in their own learning and how they can vary their pace (Quality Matters, 2013). This offers a chance for students to reinforce their understanding through retrieval. It also aids in learners' understanding of what they know and don't know so they can focus future learning.

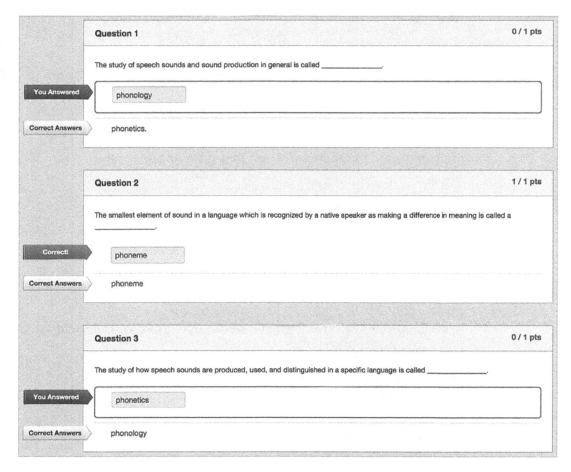

Figure 8.11 An example of a practice exercise with pop-up answers used for students to self-assess

Non-pressured low-risk forms of feedback, such as computer-generated feedback, enable learners to test their knowledge privately. Avoid specifically grading all assignments and activities. Instead, you may credit students in projects and work where the results of their reflective work have made a difference. Ungraded assessments can reduce the stress on the learners and encourage a reflective process.

 Self-correcting and/or self-assessment activities are used throughout the course to enable learners to vary the pace of their learning as is appropriate to the subject matter.

Figure 8.11 is a self-assessment from Scott Thornbury's class. It comes at the very beginning of the lesson. This gives students a sense of how much they already know about the topic.

8.7 What about Exams and Testing?

Exams and testing are common ways to assess student knowledge retention. They are appropriate ways to assess your students depending upon the subject area and/or how they are devised.

A combination of computer-corrected testing created in the test tool (see test types under practice exercises in Chapter 6) and essays can provide the instructor with a sense of the students' understanding and the ways in which they can apply their knowledge to explain, critique, assess, and discuss the course content. The idea is to provide frequent and varied assessments to ensure students are learning, and provide low-risk assessment opportunities for students.

Note on proctored exams: Your institution may require students to take a proctored exam at an exam center. This is common in courses that lead to a credential or a certification of a distinct skill set.

8.8 Summary and Standards

The standards set forth below have been discussed throughout this chapter. Use these standards to inform the design of your assessments for your online course.

Assessment

☐ The relationship between learning outcomes and assessments is evident.

☐ Assessments determine the degree to which the learners have achieved the required learning outcomes.

☐ Activities lead to active interactions that involve course content and personal communication.

☐ Course includes ongoing and frequent assessment.

☐ Self-correcting and/or self-assessment activities are used throughout the course to enable learners to vary the pace of their learning as is appropriate to the subject matter.

☐ Class participation/discussion should account for 10–30 percent of the final grade.

Evaluation and Grading

☐ Graded assignments are varied (e.g. special projects, reflective assignments, research papers, case studies, presentations, group work, etc.).

☐ Criteria and procedures for peer review and evaluation are clear.

☐ Graded elements are clearly distinguished from those that are ungraded.

☐ The relationship between graded elements and the final grade is clear.

☐ Grading criteria are outlined in the course syllabus and within the assignment or assessment itself.

☐ Students are given clear expectations and criteria for assignments. Examples are included for clarification when needed.

☐ Students can easily track their progress.

☐ Criteria/rubrics clearly inform learners as to how they will be assessed on specific assignments, such as online class participation.

Feedback

☐ Teacher, peer-to-peer, guest, and automated feedback clarifies, amplifies, and extends the topic.

☐ Teacher feedback is provided in a timely fashion.

☐ Students know when and how they will receive feedback from instructors.

Chapter 9

Building the Course Foundation: Outcomes, Syllabus, and Course Outline

This is the part of the guide that walks you through the process of building your course. The knowledge, skills, and standards groundwork have been covered. We have looked closely at what makes up a lesson. In this chapter, we will work on creating the foundation and, in Chapter 10, creating the body of the course: the presentation. The basic elements covered here are:

- learning outcomes;
- the online syllabus;
- the course outline; and
- from course outline to lessons.

9.1 The Critical Importance of Learning Outcomes

Learning outcomes are at the core of a process that creates courses that follow through on the promises made in descriptions and marketing materials for the program. There are learning outcomes expressed at every stage in the process.

Open
Openness simplifies complexity.

(Maeda, 2006); 2nd law of simplicity

We have already referred to the importance of using learning outcomes to assure learners that the online course will be as comprehensive and rigorous as its on-site equivalent. The learning outcomes for both should be identical.

They also provide the teacher with clear guidelines for developing an online course. We are therefore providing a fairly comprehensive review of what the learning outcomes are and how to write them.

Because a good number of you may already be using learning outcomes, we will not cover them in detail within this chapter. Instead, refer to Appendix A, where we provide rationales for using outcomes, the argument for using outcomes instead of objectives, and a guide for writing learning outcomes. We will, however, include **all** related standards here.

- ☑ Learning outcomes for an online course are identical to those of the on-site version.

- ☑ Learning outcomes are measurable and specific.

- ☑ The wording used to define learning outcomes is clear and definite.

- ☑ Course material is sufficient and directly related to learning outcomes.

- ☑ Resources and activities support learning outcomes.

- ☑ Assessments determine the degree to which the learners have achieved the required learning outcomes.

9.2 The Online Syllabus

An online syllabus contains many of the same elements as an on-site syllabus. The basic elements include:

- Course Title

- Course Name

- Course Description

- Course Objectives

- Evaluation Plan

- Grading

- Required Readings

- Recommended Readings

- Course Outline.

The syllabus contains a very detailed course outline, and a thorough explanation of how the online course is organized and will operate.

WEB **For a full example of an online syllabus, see the website.**

A detailed syllabus is the core organizing document for the teacher and the students. It is where students go to find out everything they need to know about the course requirements, evaluation process, contact information, schedule, and institutional policy.

Given the open flexibility of online study, it is especially important that the online syllabus be comprehensive and clear. It is the backbone of the online course. An ongoing Q&A discussion forum (see page 99) is a good place to clarify syllabus information.

The syllabus should be written to give students a good sense of the teacher's expectations for performance. When a student finishes reading the syllabus, she should have a strong idea of what it will take to achieve the course learning outcomes and succeed.

For the teacher, it is also the framework for course development. Just as students have different learning styles, teachers have different organizational, planning, and teaching styles. The process teachers use for building up a course incrementally will vary. However, the syllabus is the starting point no matter what your approach.

Special Characteristics of an Online Syllabus

We recommend that an online (vs. on-site) syllabus include additional items that are specific to online needs. These include:

- a communication strategy;

- a clear description of the course time frame and format;

- guidelines for online class participation;

- technical requirements and support; and

- a detailed course outline with start and end dates for each lesson.

Communication Strategy

A communication strategy is a description of how and when students can contact you via email, phone, chat, etc. It's important to indicate when you will return emails and phone messages (see Figure 9.1). Never underestimate how confusing and messy things can get without such a strategy.

Communication Strategy

There are several ways to contact me:

- Office Hours. I will be available for onsite office hours every Tuesday and Friday from 1pm to 3pm and online by appointment.
- By Phone Appointment. I am available for phone appointments. Please email me to schedule an appointment.
- Email. I am available by email and will respond within 24 to 48 hours. For urgent matters, I would suggest following up by phone.
- Question and Answer Discussion Forum. Always check the Question and Answer discussion forum to ask a question of the class and see if a response has been posted to your question.

Figure 9.1 An example of Kristen Sosulski's communication strategy within her online course syllabus

tip

Recommend that students set up their own profiles during the first week of class. Most LMSs let users set their own time zone, which adjusts all due dates accordingly.

Students are expected to follow the course outline and engage and participate in the activities outlined in each weekly **lesson**. Students are required to keep pace with class, follow the course outline, and complete necessary readings and assignments by the designated due date.

Example: **Due dates are expressed in day and hour EST** (Eastern Standard Time). Students are responsible for adjusting due dates to their time zone.

Course Time Frame and Format

The online course time frame is different than it is on-site. In the syllabus, clearly explain the format of the course (i.e. asynchronous) to the students. Explain that due dates and times are expressed with reference to a particular time zone (e.g. GMT, EST, etc.), usually determined by the location of the teacher. Also, describe the start date and end date for the course, and how this corresponds to the beginning and ending of each module (see Figure 9.2).

Guidelines for Class Participation

Students should be required to contribute actively for **a minimum of two to three times per week**. In some cases, the teacher may require participation within a discussion forum. Be sure to include the requirements for class participation in your syllabus and count those activities as part of the course grade (see Figure 9.3). A rubric that outlines the criteria for evaluating class participation leaves little room for confusion.

 Criteria/rubrics clearly inform learners as to how they will be assessed on specific assignments, such as online class participation.

Course Format

This course is asynchronous. We will not meet in the classroom. All activities and assignments will be completed online using the LMS.

Time Frame

You will participate when convenient within a fixed period of time, usually within a week or less (e.g. between Monday, June 1 and Sunday, June 7, 11:59pm EST).

- This is a six-week online course.
- Our online week begins on a Monday and ends on a Sunday.
- The first day of the online course is Monday, June 28 and the last day is August 4.

Figure 9.2 Course time frame and format within the online course syllabus

Participation Rubric							
Criteria	**Ratings**						**Pts**
Quality: Contributions to the online class discussion are well written, proofread, and directly relevant to the discussion topic	Exceeds Requirements 5 pts	All Met 4 pts	Mostly Met 3 pts	Somewhat Met 2 pts	Barely Met 1 pts	Not Met 0 pts	5 pts
Accuracy: All contributions are supported with evidence, if required. Sharing personal experiences is essential to this course; however, applying and referencing the salient course readings, cases, and other literature is critical.	Exceeds Requirements 5 pts	All Met 4 pts	Mostly Met 3 pts	Somewhat Met 2 pts	Barely Met 1 pts	Not Met 0 pts	5 pts
Timeliness: Contributions are made within the assigned time period.	Exceeds Requirements 5 pts	All Met 4 pts	Mostly Met 3 pts	Somewhat Met 2 pts	Barely Met 1 pts	Not Met 0 pts	5 pts
						Total Points:	15

Figure 9.3 Class participation rubric described in the course syllabus

Technical Requirements and Support

Explain to learners how they can get help if they are having trouble accessing (logging in to) the online course or using the online course tools. In addition, encourage them to be proactive and spend time learning how the course is organized in the LMS. Many institutions offer online student orientation programs; they train students on how to use the LMS. Also, refer students to the technical requirements of the LMS (see Figure 9.4). Remind students that for course content questions, they should contact the teacher.

KS: *There may be times when learners claim they had difficulties accessing the online courses, thus preventing them from fulfilling their requirements. These situations are difficult. I always ask the student for documentation from our help support (i.e. a help desk ticket) to ensure that they are taking the appropriate measures to solve their technical issues. This helps both the student and I better understand the nature of the problem and I can better assess whether the problem is one that impedes the student's ability to complete an assignment or if the issue could be attributed to a lack of preparedness, etc.*

Technical Requirements and Support

The online portion of this course will be held via the LMS. Learn more about the type of support and training provided.

For an overview on how the course works view my introductory video.

Live Online Group Meetings

Your group may want to meet online in real time. For the live online meetings, I encourage you to use Skype or Google Hangouts.

Skype: http://skype.com

Google Hangouts: https://www.google.com/+/learnmore/hangouts/

Online Technical Support

If you need assistance contact the Help Desk. They can be reached via email or phone and operate 24 hours a day.

Figure 9.4 Technical requirements within the online course syllabus

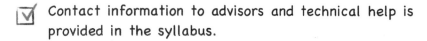 Contact information to advisors and technical help is provided in the syllabus.

KS: *For my online courses, I usually provide students with a brief two-minute video overview. In the video, I show them how the course is organized within the LMS. This includes where they can find the syllabus, course materials, how to get help, and finally the spaces I've set up for learner collaboration and communication.*

Course Outline

The online course outline is a calendar and a to-do list, and presents a sequence of:

- events;
- assignments;
- readings;
- activities; and
- course deliverables.

See Figure 9.5 for a partial online course outline from Kristen Sosulski's course. Notice how the course is organized in units and lessons. Each lesson represents one week in the online course.

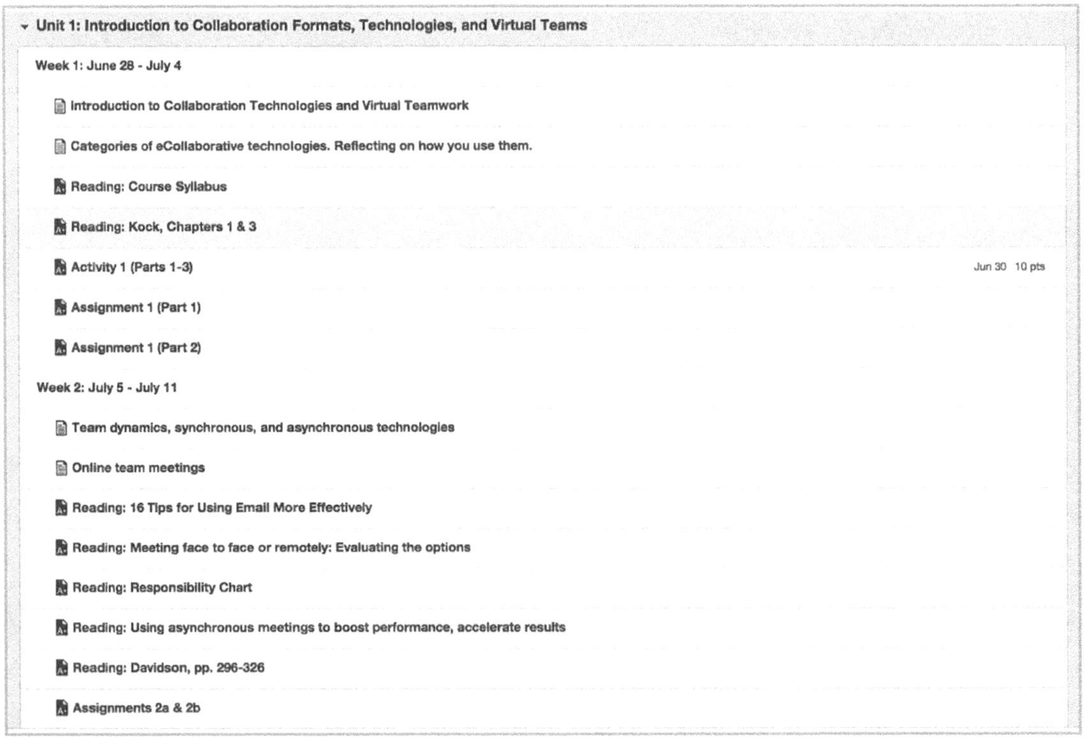

Figure 9.5 A partial example of an online course outline

Syllabus Components

The syllabus components outline below is a comprehensive checklist for the essential points that need to be covered in a syllabus and a course outline. Many items are just a carryover from the on-site syllabus.

You may find that you want to use all of the items listed here and add some. Or you may want to leave things out. For example, if your course recommends reading time-sensitive materials, you will not be able to list them ahead of time. But you can explain where the readings will come from and how much you expect the students to read. Moreover, communicate to students where they can find the information

Syllabus Components

The syllabus components outline below is a comprehensive checklist for the essential points that need to be covered in a syllabus and a course outline. Many items are just a carryover from the on-site syllabus.

Basic Course Information

- Session (e.g. Fall, 2015)
- Course title and number/section
- Instructor name and email
- Academic credits
- Prerequisite(s)

Course Time Frame and Format

- Format (i.e. **asynchronous** or **blended**, with an explanation).
- Number of weeks online.
- First and last day of the course. Note any holidays.
- Weekly start and end day for each lesson (e.g. the online week begins on Tuesday and ends on Monday).
- **Due date/time zone**: due dates are expressed in day, hour, and time zone (e.g. GMT, EST, etc.). Students are responsible for adjusting the due date to their time zone. The time zone expressed will most likely be that of the teacher (see Figure 9.2).

Course Description

This is a summary overview of the course.

Learning Outcomes

These express what the learner will know or be able to do at the end of the course.

Communication Strategy

Provides a space and place for the teacher to clearly outline his availability and response time within the online course (see Figure 9.1).

Department and Academic Advisement

This contact information connects the course with the academic program and/or department.

Technical Requirements

The contact information for online technical support and resources (see Figure 9.4).

Course Requirements

1. **Assignments.** The overview of assignments, such as number of papers, projects, participation in discussion forums, tests, quizzes, group projects, readings, etc.
2. **Assessment and Feedback Plan** (see Table 8.1).
3. **Activity grade percentages.** List how grades will be determined and the weight of each type of activity in determining a final grade.
4. **Criteria for class participation.** Students should be required to contribute to the course a minimum of two to three times per week. This may take the form of class participation activities such as online discussions. A rubric that outlines the criteria for evaluating class participation leaves little room for confusion (see Chapter 8).
5. **Policy on due dates and lateness.** Establishes clear rules and penalties for late assignments.

 The manner of submission for graded assignments is clear.

Link to Institutional Academic Policy

Statement on plagiarism, cheating, and honor code.

Course Outline

The online course outline is a calendar and to-do list, and presents a sequence of events, assignments, readings, activities, and course deliverables.

See Figure 9.5 for an example of a course outline.

they need (e.g. lessons, resources, forum, blog). **All critical information for succeeding should be in the syllabus.**

WEB A syllabus template is available on the website.

☑ All graded activities are listed upfront in the syllabus.

☑ The manner of submission for graded assignments is clear.

☑ Due dates for submissions are clear.

☑ A syllabus including contact information, a course outline, requirements, and guidelines is accessible from the start of the course and throughout.

☑ Instructions and requirements are stated simply, clearly, and logically.

☑ Consequences of missed deadlines and insufficient class participation are clearly stated and fair.

☑ The consequences of plagiarism, cheating, and failure to properly cite copyrighted material are emphasized.

9.3 Using the Course Outline as the Framework for Your Online Course

You are now set up to plan your course week by week. As we've pointed out before, a good place to start is by considering these three areas:

1. **Begin with the learning outcomes.** Each unit will have at least one learning outcome. Let's say, for example, that a learning outcome states: "The students will be able to create an organized and effective promotional slide show of a product." The lessons that make up the unit will have their own outcomes. The first in this case might be: "The students will be able to outline the qualities of an effective, promotional slide presentation on a given product."

2. **Working backwards, you next plan out what assessments you will need to assure that the learning**

outcomes have been met. The main assessment for the unit will be the completed slide show. The students will be graded on how well they do on the project. The smaller assessments for each module will build the students' skills so that they acquire the knowledge and skills they need to do the final project.

3. **Next, using the assessments as the measure of your content, you lay out the knowledge, skills, and steps needed to enable the students to succeed at the final project**—in this case, creating the professional slide show. The first module might have them look at and analyze good and bad examples of related presentations. The challenge is to now set up the activities and resources to present the knowledge and skills to the students using effective pedagogical design. Do this unit by unit within the course, lesson by lesson within each unit, and finally step by step within each section.

At this point, you should have all the background knowledge you need to do this.

 Pedagogical steps build progressively, one upon the other, as is appropriate to the subject matter.

9.4 Groundwork for Lessons

Units and lessons are really just organizing structures. The meat of the course is within the sections/segments, or the chunks within each lesson.

A Course Walk-Through

Let's look at Scott Thornbury's course on Language Analysis for Teachers. (You will see more of this course in Chapter 10.) First, look at the course description and learning outcomes in Figure 9.6.

The course has 10 units spread over 15 weeks. Most units run for one week and some for two weeks. Each unit has a specific number of lessons depending upon the natural breaks in each unit topic.

to do

Look again at the course outcomes and compare them to the unit outcomes below. Read over the items in the introduction (see Figure 9.7).

What role does each element below play in supporting the students' understanding of the course?

Now look at the section-by-section outcomes of the unit in Figure 9.8. Again, compare them first with the Unit 7 outcomes and then the overall course outcomes. This is an excellent example of the anatomy of a well-constructed course.

Language Analysis for Teachers: Phonology, Lexis, Syntax

Course Description

Language is a regularly patterned, meaning-making system. For teaching purposes, an understanding of the regularities, meanings, and underlying systems of language is an essential requirement in helping learners navigate the sometimes baffling data that they encounter.

This course explores the forms, meanings, and uses of English structure, and involves the description and analysis of the English sound system (phonology), the system of word formation (morphology), and sentence structure (syntax).

Learning Outcomes

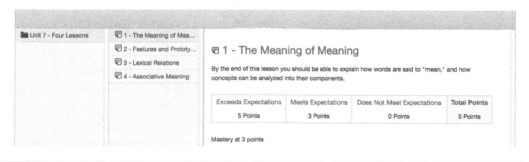

Figure 9.6 Course description and outcomes for an online course, Language Analysis for Teachers

A Unit Introduction from an Online Course

Language Analysis for Teachers: Phonology, Lexis, Syntax

Unit 7—Lexis (2): The Meaning of Words

Introduction

This unit continues the theme of lexis (vocabulary) by moving from a focus on the form of words (covered in the previous unit) to a focus on the meaning of words. In this unit, we look at theories of word meaning (or semantics), including the view that word meaning is constructed out of basic elements of meaning, and the view that our understanding of a word's meaning is represented in the form of "best examples" (or prototypes). We then look at ways that words are interrelated so that their meanings are defined in relation to other words. Finally, we look at the way words gather associations through the way they are used in social and cultural contexts.

Key Concepts

lexicon	synonym	denotation
referent	antonym	connotation
componential analysis	hyponym	register
semantic features	metonym	style
prototype	lexical set	collocation

Figure 9.7 Language Analysis for Teachers, Unit 7 Introduction

Learning Outcomes

By the end of this unit you should be able to:

- explain how words are said to "mean," and how concepts can be analyzed into their components;
- explain the role that prototypes play in assigning word meaning;
- describe the main ways in which word meaning is defined in relation to other words; and
- identify different ways that words are "colored" by their associations.

Unit 7 has four lessons:

1. The meaning of meaning
2. Features and prototypes (see pages 195–199)
3. Lexical relations
4. Associative meaning

Each of the above lessons contains readings, tasks, and assignments to complete. Please complete the lessons sequentially.

These are the main tasks you will be asked to do in this unit:

Discussion Board Tasks

- Compare differences between prototypical examples of different categories (not assessed).
- Evaluate the teacher's explanations of words (assessed).
- Discuss the validity of translating words from L2 to L1 (assessed).

Written Task

- Find a text and analyze its lexical content from three different points of view (assessed).

Figure 9.7 Continued

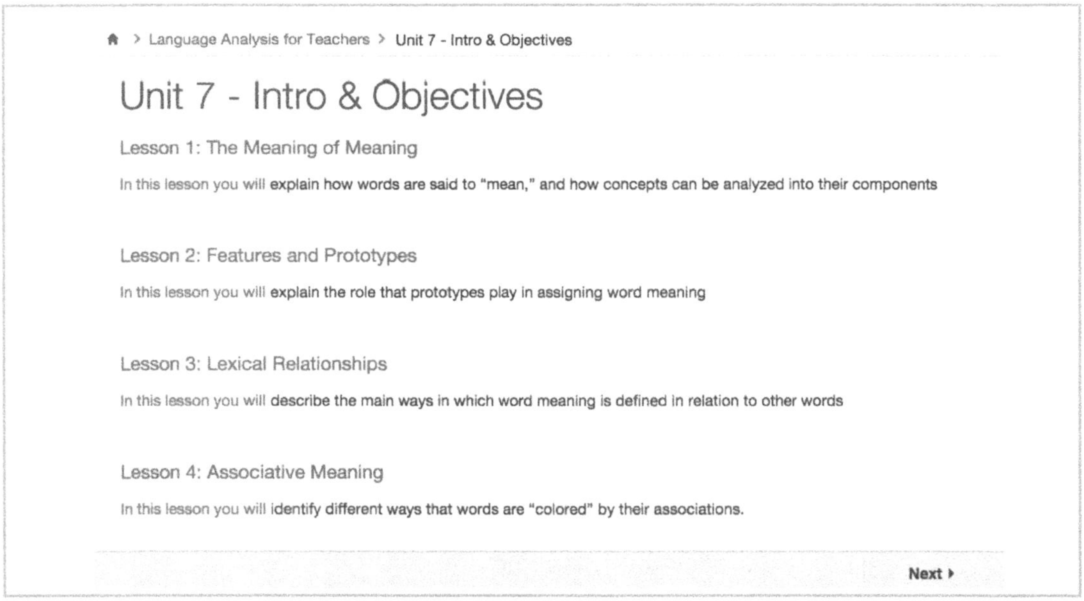

Figure 9.8 An online unit with four lessons and sets of learning outcomes

Here again, we will have the featured teacher describe his process in his own voice. Again, when Scott is speaking, the text will be in italics and begin with "ST:"

ST: *This course—like many graduate courses—involves a fairly hefty load of terminology, and what I wanted to do was flag these as soon as possible—in the form of "key concepts" in the overview section of each module (see Figure 9.7). In this way, they provide a kind of schematic summary, or "advance organizer," of what students can expect to encounter as they work through the module. Also, for review purposes, I think it's helpful to have all the key terms in one place. (Incidentally, paying this much attention to the terminology in the design of the online course has made me much more aware of the importance of flagging these terms when I teach the course face to face.)*

☑ **Introductions and summaries are provided at the beginning and end of units.**

The website provides templates on each stage of this process.

ST: *Assessment is, unsurprisingly, the area that causes students the most anxiety. So I don't think you can be too explicit as to what it is the students have to do, how this will be assessed, and how much it counts toward their final grade. In terms of telling students what you have to do, I have found that nothing works better than an example, and over time I have saved examples of previous students' work, which I make available as a model. Of course, simply copying the model is not an option!*

See Figure 9.9 for Scott Thornbury's explanation of how assessment is broken down.

 All graded activities are listed upfront in the syllabus.

Assessment

Course Requirement	Specifications	Words (approximately)	Value
1	Discussion board participation		30
2	8 assignments @ 5 points each	8 × 500 = 4000	35
3	2 longer assignments submitted at ends of weeks 8 and 12: 1500 words each	3000	35
	Total:	**7000**	**100**

Figure 9.9 An example of the course assessment section of the online syllabus

9.5 Summary and Standards

In this chapter, we have looked at the elements of an online course and its stages of development. We have paid special attention to the development of the learning outcomes and the online syllabus, including a detailed course outline. Once you have completed this foundation, you can move on to designing the lessons for the course.

☐ Learning outcomes for an online course are identical to those of the on-site version.

☐ Learning outcomes are measurable and specific.

☐ The wording used to define learning outcomes is clear and definite.

☐ Course material is sufficient and directly related to learning outcomes.

☐ Resources and activities support learning outcomes.

☐ Assessments determine the degree to which the learners have achieved the required learning outcomes.

☐ Criteria/rubrics clearly inform learners as to how they will be assessed on specific assignments, such as online class participation.

☐ Contact information to advisors and technical help is provided in the syllabus.

☐ All graded activities are listed upfront in the syllabus.

☐ A syllabus including contact information, a course outline, requirements, and guidelines is accessible from the start of the course and throughout.

☐ Instructions and requirements are stated simply, clearly, and logically.

☐ Due dates for submissions are clear.

☐ The manner of submission for graded assignments is clear.

☐ Consequences of missed deadlines and insufficient class participation are clearly stated and fair.

☐ The consequences of plagiarism, cheating, and failure to properly cite copyrighted material are emphasized.

☐ Pedagogical steps build progressively, one upon the other, as is appropriate to the subject matter.

☐ Introductions and summaries are provided at the beginning and end of units.

Chapter 10 Structuring the Course Content: The Online Presentation

Let's now look at how the material covered in Chapters 6–9 leads to an online presentation.

10.1 Designing Engaging Content

Text-based lectures, whether in writing, audio, or video, are passive or receptive. To make the presentation of new knowledge active or productive, develop a varied series of activities so that students interact with each other, the teacher, and the content. Have them analyze, combine, choose, create, collaborate, test themselves, explore, synthesize, reflect, etc.

There are many ways to create the kind of textured environment that keeps learners involved and interested.

 to do

Use the following ideas to begin brainstorming

- Transform materials into activities. Use different types of readings, and ask students to categorize, eliminate, question, add to, redesign, extend, etc. as is appropriate. Turn things on their heads. Provide solutions and have students identify the problem (see Chapter 6).

- Incorporate varied media (see Chapter 7). The presentation of new knowledge and skills can come in many forms and combinations. Think of using, as is appropriate for the class you are designing: images, brief audio/video lectures, text-/image-/video-based slide shows, or written narratives. Multimedia learning can aid students in remembering and understanding the course content (Mayer, 2001). Use carefully chosen media resources with focused tasks to present new concepts.

- Change the presenters—alternate student or other voices with your own (see Chapter 7).

- Reference and include resources from different sources, including libraries, the Internet, databases, interviews, etc. (see Chapter 7).

- Use a mix of setups—incorporate collaborative activities or shift responsibilities to the students (see Chapter 6).

- Provide frequent opportunities for reflection and self-assessment (see Chapter 8). Reflective activities, and self-assessment mixed in with activities, motivate the students by letting them know where they are in the process. They can also recycle information in a different context thus strengthening understanding.

Set out a plan for staging the lesson. Will they begin the week with a reading or an activity? Then what? Identify where it is necessary for you to add explanations to support learning. How will you help them pace their learning? How will you assess learning?

Before beginning with the presentation, students will have seen the introduction to the unit and the outcomes. The learning outcomes are measurable and the content is directly related to the learning outcomes. They have been given an outline of what they will cover and what is expected of them (see Figure 9.6).

 Course material is sufficient and directly related to learning outcomes.

☑ Learning outcomes are measurable and specific.

Breaking up Material into Chunks or Subtopics

Part of what we do as teachers is present new information to students. But how do we best do that online? Posting long lecture notes or a long video of a lecture online is not the most effective way to present new information to students. We have learned with time and research that students find such unbroken density in content very difficult to deal with online.

At the most basic level, online content must be broken up. You may have heard this referred to as "chunking." Chunking does not just mean that you break up text into shorter paragraphs. It means that the presentation is broken down into a series of mini-presentations.

 Blocks of information are broken up or "chunked" into incremental learning sections, segments, or steps as is appropriate to the subject matter.

Use of Text, Images, and Multimedia

A great deal of variety can be achieved by putting together a mix of different learning materials, including text-based segments, short readings, images, diagrams, or multimedia from the Web. Intersperse this content with reflections, brief discussions, or self-assessments that give learners the opportunity to apply their knowledge. This approach also offers opportunities to develop a range of thinking skills.

> Learners can better understand an explanation when it is presented in words and pictures than when it is presented in words only.
>
> (Mayer, 2001, p. 1)

In the best cases, mini-lectures are varied in design and presentation. Depending upon the content area, charts, photos, illustrations, links, and audio and video are used to create a textured, multifaceted environment. The purposeful development of content in different ways, and from different perspectives, clarifies and extends understanding.

However, when variety is used gratuitously (i.e. variety for the sake of variety), it can distract and even detract. For example, presenting text slides along with narration interferes with understanding. This type of simultaneous redundancy impedes learning (Mayer, 2001). It is best to keep things both varied and simple at the same time.

Be open to new ways of communication that cut down on your dependency on text as the sole means of presenting information. If you are comfortable with speaking, for example, include some brief audio or video clips of you explaining or demonstrating something.

☑ Courses include a variety of relevant multimedia to support learning (e.g. audio, video, recommended podcasts, illustrations, photographs, charts, and graphs).

☑ Content is designed simply and clearly to avoid information overload (e.g. avoid narrating while written text is visible, using distracting images for decoration, presenting too much information at once, etc.).

☑ Details in images, graphs, charts, and diagrams are designed and organized so that they are easy to read and understand.

Before we walk you through a presentation, let's first review some standards that are particularly important at this point:

☑ Presentations, activities, and assessments address a variety of learning abilities and preferences.

☑ The manner of presenting new knowledge and skills is varied, including text, lists, organizational activities, reflective quizzes, readings, images, graphs, charts, etc.

☑ Presentations include examples, models, case studies, illustrations, etc. for clarification.

☑ Materials are authentic or relate to real-life applications.

☑ Topics and materials are up to date and relevant.

☑ Presentations include media and are varied.

☑ Activities engage students in higher-level thinking skills, including critical and creative thinking, analysis, and problem-solving.

☑ Reflection and reflective activities come up throughout the course.

☑ Activities lead to active interactions that involve course content and personal communication.

10.2 The Presentation: Introducing and Reinforcing Knowledge

We will now look at a presentation from one of our featured teachers, Scott Thornbury. This presentation comes up in the middle of a unit (see Figure 9.8).

Language Analysis

Lesson 7, Section 2—Scott Thornbury

ST: *The course I designed was aimed at teachers of English as a second or foreign language, as part of a Master's program, taught either online or (optionally) on-site. This particular course deals with aspects of the language knowledge base required to teach the English language, including grammar, vocabulary, and phonology. There are 10 modules overall, normally spread over a 15-week semester.*

What I was trying to do in this module was take a rather tricky area (i.e. semantics) and "package" it in such a way that: (a) it wasn't too dense and forbidding; and (b) it drew out the practical applications for language teaching. This meant designing the unit so that it was a succession of small steps: a progression of short readings, interspersed with reflective tasks and discussions, and with lots of graphics both to break up the text and (importantly!) to illustrate the content.

(In revising this unit subsequently, and in the interests of reducing the text load, I added a spoken slide presentation).

Let's first look at some details from the first section in lesson 7, "The Meaning of Meaning." Here's the outcome:

By the end of this section, you should be able to explain how words are said to "mean," and how concepts can be analyzed into their components.

ST: *One of the concepts introduced here is componential analysis.*

Theorists have attempted to break down concepts into "atoms" of meaning, using what is called "componential analysis." The underlying principle of componential analysis is that all words can be analyzed using a finite set of components.

 # to do

At this point, we have covered the basic components and gone through the standards for presenting new knowledge and skills. Let's examine what we know through this example.

As we go through the lesson, we will periodically pose questions. Why we are asking the questions may be obvious. Our point is to have you reflect on how these points have been dealt with in an online environment.

We suggest that you go through this lesson twice as follows:

First time: Go through the lesson imagining that you are the student. Do not read the questions that appear in this gray between the boxed sections of the lesson. Instead, think about these:

- Was the writing clear?

- Were the pictures helpful?

- Were the things you were asked to do helpful?

- Imagine if this were all text with no visuals and no tasks/activities. What would that have been like?

Second time: Read the questions in this gray posed between the sections. These will help you analyze the module as a teacher.

What does the learning outcome tell you and how is that helpful?

What is covered in the short introductory statement?
1 . . . 2 . . . 3 . . .

> ### Learning Outcome
> By the end of this section you should be able to explain the role that prototypes play in assigning word meaning.

In the previous section we saw how componential analysis attempts to explain how the meaning of a word is composed, or constructed, from simpler meanings. However, the quest for the definitive semantic features of a concept, even a concept as simple as table, is not easy. How can we be sure that we have only those features that are common to all tables? Here, for example, is a componential analysis of the word chair:

Chair (object), (physical), (non-living), (artifact), (furniture), (portable), (something with legs), (something with a back), (something with a seat), (seat for one)

Figure 10.1 Outcome from Scott Thornbury's class

What is Scott asking students to do in task 7.2.1 in Figure 10.2?

Think of Bloom's hierarchy (see Appendix A). What levels of thinking skills are being dealt with here?

Task 7.2.1

1. Can you think of examples of *chair* (in its meaning as a piece of furniture) that don't fit the above analysis? Here are some pictures of chairs. Which fit/don't fit the analysis? Could you improve on the analysis?

Figure 10.2 Lesson 2, task 1, part 1

How does the second part of this task in Figure 10.3 differ
from the first? Is there a progression?

2. Attempt to analyze the concept of *table* in the same way. Here are some pictures of tables that might help:

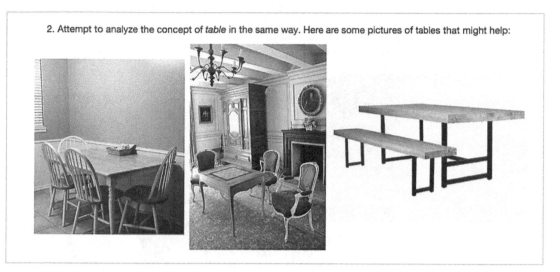

Figure 10.3 Lesson 2, task 1, part 2

Now, listen to the course author talking about this task.

The difficulty in identifying the necessary and sufficient "atoms" of meaning that are common to all members of such broad categories as, say, chairs or tables, has led some theorists to question the view that word meanings are simple the combination of a finite number of semantic features. Moreover, word meanings are often quite "fuzzy" at the edges, with the meaning of one word "leaking" into the meaning of different but related words. In one famous experiment, the sociolinguist Labov asked informants to name various containers.

"They not only disagree with one another over bowls, cups and vases, but were inconsistent from day to day. Certain shapes were clear in instances of particular containers, but others varied: something might be a bowl when full of potatoes, but a vase when it held flowers" (Aitchison, 1997, 65).

Figure 10.4 Audio segment—Scott Thornbury discusses the task in Figures 10.2 and 10.3
(text at bottom)

WEB What purposes might the audio serve at this point? You can listen to it on the website.

Task 2

Test yourself: which of the following would you classify as a cup, mug, bowl, or vase (or none of the above!)?

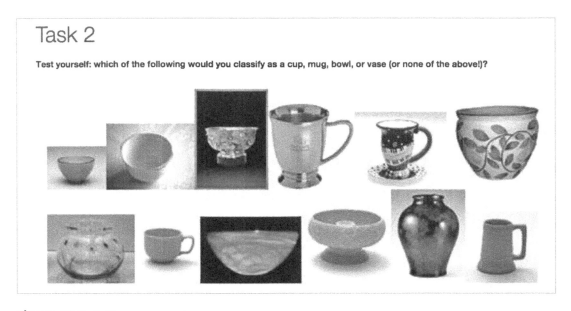

Figure 10.5 Self-assessment

note

Notice the marks around the term **Prototype theory** in **Fig. 10.6.** These indicate that this is one of the key concepts covered in the introduction.

What simple yet critical piece of information is added in the short statement in Figure 10.4?

What purpose does this self-assessment serve (see Figure 10.5)?

At this point, think about what the student has learned.

How has the topic evolved (see Figures 10.2–10.6)?

This is an international class with members from many different locations around the globe. How engaged do you imagine an international class will be in the following discussion board activity?

From the above activity, it should be clear that we don't rank all examples of a category as being equally representative. Some examples are more "typical" than others. <**Prototype theory**> argues that we understand the meaning of a word by reference to these typical—or "best"—examples. These best examples are used by the mind as a way of assessing whether marginal or doubtful examples belong to the same category. As Schmitt (2000) points out, our notion of what might be a best example of a category is partly culturally determined:

> Rosch (1975) found that people within a culture tend to have a relatively uniform idea of what the best examples are. For instance, Americans considered robins to be the best example of a bird, because robins represent the attributes people most commonly associate with birdiness: for example, flying, laying eggs, building nests, and singing. When compared to robins, penguins and ostriches had enough of these 'birdy' features to be considered birds, although not typical ones. Although bats fly, they did not have enough other features to be considered birds (p. 25).

Figure 10.6 An explanation/chunk

Unit 7: DB1 Prototypes
Scott Thornbury

Dec 2 at 1:38pm

4

What - to you - is the "best example" of the following categories? How might your choice differ from that of a person from another culture that you are familiar with?

1. flower
2. vegetable
3. vehicle
4. dwelling
5. sport
6. woman's clothing
7. musical instrument
8. profession

(This discussion is NOT assessed.)

Figure 10.7 A topical discussion activity

ST: *Here are some of the qualities you might have noticed in this lesson:*

- *The learning outcomes clearly describe the purpose of the lesson.*

- *I have tried to break up, or chunk, the lesson into a series of sections designed to keep students moving forward, step by step, and engaged.*

- *There is a minimum of text, either explanatory or commentary, on the tasks.*

- *The tone straddles the academic (citations are correctly referenced) and informal, even conversational, with a minimum of jargon—the terminology is explained as I go along. Note that I use British English, being a native of New Zealand, but without any overt regional features so that it is broadly comprehensible across a range of varieties of English.*

- *The images in this presentation break up the space and provide white space. When introducing challenging content, such space helps focus attention. As John Maeda points out: "The opportunity lost by increasing the amount of blank space is gained back with enhanced attention to what remains" (Maeda, 2006, p. 56).*

 ## to do

Review Scott Thornbury's presentation in terms of the checklist of standards at the end of this chapter.

 The examples of the work from our featured teachers is available on the website. The best way to proceed with this exercise is to view the examples on the website while you go through the standards.

10.3 DIY: Do It Yourself

Following are a variety of lists, charts, and suggestions for you to refer to when working through a lesson. Use all or only those that best suit you.

Let's look again at the segments in a lesson:

- Outcome

- Introduction

- Activity

- Activity

- Activity

- . . .

- Summary

  to do

WEB **A template for designing lessons can be downloaded from the website.** Why not take some time to brainstorm on the following:

1. Decide how many sections you need to cover the topic of your lesson. Remember, skills-based courses usually need to be broken up into small steps that build upon one another. Consequently, you may need to group them into a few sections/sub-topics. Once you have defined the topic or sub-topic for a section, the next two steps (2 and 3) are straightforward.

2. Write the learning outcome(s).

3. Write the introduction.

4. Analyze and break up your content into a series of segments or "chunks" that make sense.

5. Review the material and see where or how it might be enhanced by images, charts, graphs, etc. Can any of the chunks of information be transformed into or supported by audio or video? Would linking to a resource expand the content in a meaningful way?

6. Activities, activities, activities. Determine how and where within each lesson there will be points for students to engage with the content, each other, the teacher, experts, and in individual and group activities. Remember, self-assessments are activities.

As a quick reference, look over this list for activity ideas:

- Activities such as practice exercises, online discussions, etc. (see Chapter 6). Which?

- Assigned readings with guidelines. What kinds of guidelines might you set up to make readings more interactive and challenging?

- Assigned research-based student presentations. Where is the research done? What do students do with the results? Do they present them as is, or transform or combine them in some way? Do they do these alone or in collaboration with other class members? Who and how many others?

- Periodic self-assessments and reflective activities. How often? (see Chapter 6).

- Guest speakers. Who? Why? How? What is the relationship to the topic? Who provides feedback?

- Experiences from the field. Who? What? How? In what form? What is the feedback? Who provides it?

- Assigned reports on real-life research such as surveys and interviews.

- Brief audio and video clips (two to five minutes). Ready-made, teacher-made, or student-made?

- Student presentations. Individuals or groups?

10.4 Building the Course in the LMS

There are several tactics you may take when designing your course.

Identify the resources for course development at your institution, if any. First, check to see if your institution provides resources to support the creation of multimedia elements for your course. Institutions with larger online programs typically have entire departments dedicated to online teaching and learning. These departments have talented

Storyboard
A sequence of drawings or descriptions of images with directions used to plan out shots for a video.

individuals who are skilled in this in various types of production and educational design. In working with these groups, you may need to plan your entire course well in advance of the course start date, especially if your course requires video lessons. Videos take time to storyboard, record, and edit. Even without those resources, it is still possible for a teacher to create great multimedia resources by following the basic design standards in Chapters 3, 4, and 7.

Learn how to use the LMS. Find help through your institution, read online resources, and try creating a sample lesson within it. Where do you find the LMS reaches its limits? Where do you need to extend the capabilities through the use of other collaborative tools (e.g. Google Docs), communication tools (e.g. Skype, Google Hangouts), or sharing tools (e.g. Google Drive, DropBox)?

Create a structure for your lessons. It's helpful to create a prototype lesson that you can use as a template for the remainder of the lessons. Also, usually the first week of the course is different than the remaining weeks; people are getting to know each other during the first week, etc.

10.5　Summary and Standards

tip
For those of you who are new to teaching online, don't try to do it all at once. Focus on a limited set of techniques the first time out. See what works for you. Then you can enhance the work you have done and adjust the course each time you teach it, if you need to.

At this point, you have all you need to create engaging, pedagogically sound online presentations, lessons, resources, activities, and a syllabus. The basic principles have been covered. The exercise of comparing the example lessons to the entire list of standards should have set the standards in your mind.

This is the end of the online course design process. When your course goes live, this is where the teaching begins. During this time, you'll be making weekly announcements, participating in and monitoring online discussions, providing feedback on course assignments and activities, structuring group activities (such as putting students into teams—something that cannot be done prior to the class beginning), asking your students for feedback on the course design, pace, and structure, and finally communicating with students regularly to ensure a well-engaged online classroom.

 References will be provided on the website to resources that can guide you in your online teaching.

Note: The third book in this series, *Essentials of Online Teaching: A Standards-Based Guide*, picks up where this book leaves off. It guides you through the process of teaching an online course.

- [ ] Learning outcomes are measurable and specific.

- [ ] Course material is sufficient and directly related to learning outcomes.

- [ ] The manner of presenting new knowledge and skills is varied, including text, lists, organizational activities, reflective quizzes, readings, images, graphs, charts, etc.

- [ ] Presentations include examples, models, case studies, illustrations, etc. for clarification.

- [ ] Materials are authentic or relate to real-life applications.

- [ ] Topics and materials are up to date and relevant.

- [ ] Presentations include media and are varied.

- [ ] Presentations, activities, and assessments address a variety of learning abilities and preferences.

- [ ] Activities engage students in higher-level thinking skills, including critical and creative thinking, analysis, and problem-solving.

- [ ] Reflection and reflective activities come up throughout the course.

- [ ] Activities lead to active interactions that involve course content and personal communication.

- [ ] Blocks of information are broken up or "chunked" into incremental learning sections, segments, or steps as is appropriate to the subject matter.

☐ Courses include a variety of relevant multimedia to support learning (e.g. audio, video, recommended podcasts, illustrations, photographs, charts, and graphs).

☐ Content is designed simply and clearly to avoid information overload (e.g. avoid narrating while written text is visible, using distracting images for decoration, presenting too much information at once, etc.).

☐ Details in images, graphs, charts, and diagrams are designed and organized so that they are easy to read and understand.

Appendix A Writing Learning Outcomes

A.1 Learning Outcomes Support Online Course Development

Used deliberately and carefully, learning outcomes become powerful tools for defining the development of an online learning module.

The care you put into the thoughtful writing of and follow-through on learning outcomes is key to assuring that the online course matches the on-site equivalent in content and challenge.

Outcomes keep programs and courses on track.

Programs intended to be practical professional preparation, for example, may devote too much time to theory and not enough to applied practice. Outcomes can keep the practical in sight.

In skills-based courses, such as math and languages, outcomes can assure that learners move smoothly through levels of acquisition and expertise.

While there is some debate on the use of outcomes in the humanities, they can and should be used. Here also, learning outcomes assure learners that they have acquired the skills, knowledge, and an understanding of thinking processes involved in analysis, evaluation, and creation.

Outcomes motivate. Because online study is more flexible than on-site, it appeals to special segments of the population that need to fit study into their busy schedule. Most cannot afford to waste money, time, or energy. Outcomes provide clearly communicated expectations for what a course will enable them to do. As such, outcomes can reassure and motivate learners. Furthermore, they enable learners to evaluate their course.

A.2 Outcomes vs. Objectives

The terms "outcomes" and "objectives" are often used interchangeably. However, there is an implied difference in the two. **Objectives** outline goals for the teacher to reach in a learning segment. They are **teacher-focused**.

Outcomes speak of a change in the learner. Learning outcomes are stated in terms of what the learner will know or be able to do if he has successfully completed a unit. As such, they are **learner-centered**. At the very least, objectives should be written after the learning outcomes to help the teacher meet them.

Expressing goals in outcomes is very motivating for the learner. For example, assume that this guide is being used in a staff development training group. One outcome would be **"You will be able to identify and provide examples of the standards and techniques used to design effective online courses."** This tells you that you are acquiring knowledge and skills that will get you to your goal (provided that you meet the requirements set out).

Universities and schools increasingly require that academic achievement be determined in terms of learning outcomes. It is terrific public relations for a teacher, trainer, program, or institution to declare that they can provide a specific set of skills and/or a specific level of academic achievement for their learners. This provides a check on the program. Educational institutions and companies that deliver on their promises graduate learners of a quality that fully supports their success in their chosen field or profession.

The three most challenging steps when devising and using learning outcomes are:

* writing them;

* assuring that you have provided all the course material and activities needed for achieving them; and

* assessing that the outcomes have been achieved.

A.3 Rationales for Writing Learning Outcomes

A learning outcome states what the learner will know or be able to do at the end of a learning unit. The unit may be a segment, a module, or even the course itself.

Well-written learning outcomes:

- are specific;

- are clearly and concisely written;

- clarify for learners why they are doing what they are doing;

- support and help to provide a framework for the online development process by:

  - defining the knowledge and/or skills to be acquired;
  - helping to determine the content and activities for the course by pointing to the kinds of thinking skills needed; and
  - providing goals for assessment;

- help to insure the quality of the course; and

- set up an agreement between teacher and learner as to their relative responsibilities.

A.4 How to Write Clear, Concise Learning Outcomes

The first step is to focus on the verbs used in learning outcomes. The classification of levels of thinking directly informs the choice of verbs. So, let's start there.

Classifying Levels of Thinking

Benjamin Bloom classified the order of the development of higher thinking skills. Bloom's *Taxonomy of Educational Objectives* (1956) has been used to describe the progressive development of higher-ordered thinking skills for more than 50 years.

Here's how it works. At the first level (the bottom of Figure A.1), the learner knows about or remembers a concept. Now she can move to the next step: understanding the concept. Next, she can work on applying what she understands.

About 20 years ago, a student of Bloom's, Lorin Anderson, revised the taxonomy using verb forms instead of nouns to explain the process. Also, the top two categories were revised. This revised approach is on the right column of Figure A.1.

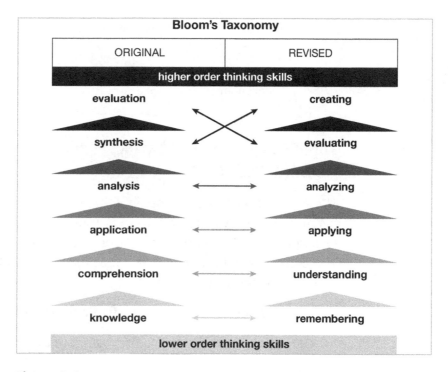

Figure A.1 Bloom's taxonomy

Using Active Verbs

Because outcomes usually describe something the learner will be able to do, they are described using active verbs. For example, specific active verbs such as "match," "locate," or "describe" would be used instead of "understand." Each order of thinking skills has certain measurable active verbs associated with it. Figure A.2 provides some examples.

Thinking skills	Active, specific verbs
creating	Plan, assemble, construct, develop, design, create...
evaluating	Appraise, judge, edit, rate, debate, estimate, interpret...
analyzing	Differentiate, classify, infer, categorize, analyze, calculate, contrast, compare...
applying	Demonstrate, modify, prepare, produce, show, paint, use, sketch, illustrate, teach...
understanding	Estimate, explain, give examples, paraphrase, explain why, summarize, recognize
remembering	Describe, identify, list, name, outline, select, match.

Figure A.2 The active verbs associated with the revised Bloom's taxonomy

Three Components: Behavior, Conditions, Measurable Criteria

The most common way to begin writing a learning outcome is by stating, "You will be able to . . ." thus indicating a change or acquisition of skills or behavior on the part of the learner. The challenge is to be sure that what follows this phrase is definite and the verb is active.

Learning outcomes include these two components:

- **Behavior.** What will the learner be able to do?

- **Conditions.** How will the learner be able to do it?

However, a third component is implied:

- **Measurable criteria.** How well will the learner be able to do it? Or, what is the minimum level of achievement acceptable to deem learner performance acceptable for achieving the outcome?

Clearly, if the student does not do her part in the learning process, she will not end up "being able to do" what is laid out in the learning outcome. Her grade indicates the extent to which she has achieved the learning or acquisition set out.

Figure A.3 sets up a format for writing learning outcomes. The measurable criteria are assured by using verbs that indicate a measurable aspect of learning.

Notice that Figure A.3 contains the two core components of a learning outcome. How measurable criteria are determined will be covered in the evaluation plan syllabus.

explain how......	in a 10 minute video presentation	see syllabus
describe the process......	in a paper, no more than 200 words	see syllabus
show how......	in a three page report	see syllabus
outline......	in a lesson plan	see syllabus
analyze......	in writing on discussion forum	see syllabus

Figure A.3 Components of a real learning outcome

Well-written learning outcomes act as a guide and double check for the following standards:

 Learning outcomes are measurable and specific.

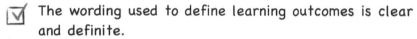 The wording used to define learning outcomes is clear and definite.

A.5 Resources

- "Bloom's Taxonomy—Bloom's Digital Taxonomy": www.techlearning.com/techlearning/archives/2008/04/AndrewChurches.pdf

- "Writing Learning Outcomes—Oxford Brooks University" (some suggestions): www.brookes.ac.uk/services/ocsd/2_learntch/writing_learning_outcomes.html

- Self-correcting quiz on Bloom's taxonomy: http://school.discoveryeducation.com/quizzes22/honglin/LearningOutcomes.html

Using the Standards Checklist

Standards encourage consistency, clear learner expectations, and overall quality and design principles across the program. This list also serves as a standards index. Each standard is followed by the page number(s) it appears on within the chapters.

B.1 Learning Outcomes

☐ 1. Learning outcomes for an online course are identical to those of the on-site version. (23, 172) [C1, C9]

☐ 2. Learning outcomes are measurable and specific. (172, 191, 211) [C9, C10, A]

☐ 3. Course material is sufficient and directly related to learning outcomes. (23, 172, 191) [C1, C9, C10]

☐ 4. Resources and activities support learning outcomes. (94, 172) [C6, C9]

☐ 5. Assessments determine the degree to which the learners have achieved the required learning outcomes. (153, 172) [C8, C9]

B.2 Ease of Communication

☐ 1. The writing style is clear, concise, and direct. (50) [C3]

☐ 2. Sentences and paragraphs are brief and to the point. (50) [C3]

☐ 3. Familiar or common words are used when possible. (52) [C3]

☐ 4. Jargon, clichés, and colloquial and idiomatic expressions are avoided. (52) [C3]

☐ 5. The meaning of special terms, abbreviations, and acronyms is easy to access. (53) [C3]

☐ 6. Labeling in all presentation materials is accurate, readable, and clear. (56, 136) [C3, C7]

☐ 7. The wording used to define learning outcomes is clear and definite. (172, 211) [C9, A1]

☐ 8. Instructions and requirements are stated simply, clearly, and logically. (54, 181) [C3, C9]

☐ 9. A supportive second-person conversational tone is used throughout the course. (53) [C3]

☐ 10. The course material has been edited for language and grammar. (57) [C3]

☐ 11. The pacing of spoken language is natural sounding yet slow enough to be understood by a variety of learners. (57) [C3]

☐ 12. The sound quality of audio and video is good enough to be clearly understood. (57) [C3]

☐ 13. Avoid combining spoken and written narrative in presentations. (73) [C4]

☐ 14. Videos should be no longer than 10 minutes in length. (74) [C4]

B.3 Pedagogical and Organizational Design

☐ 1. A syllabus including contact information, a course outline, requirements, and guidelines is accessible from the start of the course and throughout. (181) [C9]

☐ 2. Introductions and summaries are provided at the beginning and end of units. (186) [C9]

☐ 3. Blocks of information are broken up or "chunked" into incremental learning sections, segments, or steps as is appropriate to the subject matter. (192) [C10]

☐ 4. Pedagogical steps build progressively, one upon the other, as is appropriate to the subject matter. (182) [C9]

B.4 Visual Design

☐ 1. Page layout is uncluttered and open, and includes a significant amount of white space. (61) [C4]

☐ 2. There is sufficient space between lines, paragraphs, and to the right and left of text so that it stands out and is easy to read. (62) [C4]

☐ 3. Text is left-justified and right margins are ragged. (63) [C4]

☐ 4. Headings and subheadings are used consistently to logically organize content. (63) [C4]

☐ 5. A universal sans serif Web typeface (e.g. Verdana) assures access across platforms and enhances screen readability. (65) [C4]

☐ 6. Type size should be large enough to be easily readable by all students. (65) [C4]

☐ 7. Bold and italic typefaces are used sparingly only to emphasize important items. (65) [C4]

☐ 8. Underlining is used only for links. (65) [C4]

☐ 9. Words in all caps are avoided. (65) [C4]

☐ 10. Color is used with purpose. (67) [C4]

☐ 11. There is good contrast between text and background. (67) [C4]

☐ 12. Visual elements (e.g. icons, shading, and color) are used consistently to distinguish between different types of course elements (e.g. lessons, assignments, audio, and video). (68) [C4]

☐ 13. Use bullets or numbers to set apart items that can be listed. (68) [C4]

☐ 14. Numbers are used to identify sequential steps in a task or process. They are also used for rankings and setting priorities. (68) [C4]

☐ 15. Bullets are used to highlight a series of items that are not prioritized or sequential. (68) [C4]

☐ 16. Details in images, graphs, charts, and diagrams are designed and organized so that they are easy to read and understand. (136, 193) [C7, C10]

☐ 17. Content is designed simply and clearly to avoid information overload (e.g. avoid narrating while written text is visible, using distracting images for decoration, presenting too much information at once, etc.). (73, 193) [C4, C10]

B.5 Engaged Learning

☐ 1. Course content is designed to encourage interactions between learners. (94) [C6]

☐ 2. Presentations, activities, and assessments address a variety of learning abilities and preferences. (83, 146, 193) [C5, C7, C10]

☐ 3. Presentations include examples, models, case studies, illustrations, etc. for clarification. (193) [C10]

☐ 4. Materials are authentic or relate to real-life applications. (146, 193) [C7, C10]

☐ 5. The manner of presenting new knowledge and skills is varied, including text, lists, organizational activities, reflective quizzes, readings, images, graphs, charts, etc. (193) [C10]

☐ 6. Courses include a variety of relevant multimedia to support learning (e.g. audio, video, recommended podcasts, illustrations, photographs, charts, and graphs). (133, 193) [C7, C10]

☐ 7. Presentations include media and are varied. (193) [C10]

☐ 8. Activities are frequent and varied. Students may respond to questions, select options, provide information, or interact with others. (94) [C6]

☐ 9. Activities engage students in higher-level thinking skills, including critical and creative thinking, analysis, and problem-solving. (94, 193) [C6, C10]

☐ 10. Activities lead to active interactions that involve course content and personal communication. (153, 193) [C8, C10]

☐ 11. Topics and materials are up to date and relevant. (146, 193) [C7, C10]

☐ 12. Reflection and reflective activities come up throughout the course. (193) [C10]

☐ 13. Bibliographies and reference lists include a variety of resources, including Web links, books, journals, video, and downloadable text and audio files as is appropriate. (147) [C7]

B.6 Learning Interactions and Community

☐ 1. There are sufficient opportunities for learners to work collaboratively. (125) [C6]

☐ 2. Online spaces (e.g. discussion boards, social networks) are in place for students to participate in and meet outside the class. (98) [C6]

☐ 3. Learners take responsibility for their learning and, at times, the learning of others. (85) [C5]

☐ 4. The teacher is a participant in the learning process. (83) [C5]

☐ 5. Learners are encouraged to interact with others (fellow classmates, course guests, etc.) and benefit from their experience and expertise. (89, 125, 142) [C5, C6, C7]

☐ 6. Class participation activities (e.g. discussion boards, wikis, social networks) are used to build community. (87) [C5]

☐ 7. Procedures for group activities are specified so that students are aware of their role and responsibility in collaborative activities. (89, 125) [C5, C6]

☐ 8. Collaborative activities are designed to facilitate a safe learning environment. (89) [C5]

☐ 9. Students work in a variety of independent and collaborative configurations that reflect real-world situations. (87) [C5]

B.7 Assessment

☐ 1. The relationship between learning outcomes and assessments is evident. (153) [C8]

☐ 2. Course includes ongoing and frequent assessment. (154) [C8]

☐ 3. Students are given clear expectations and criteria for assignments. Examples are included for clarification when needed. (161) [C8]

☐ 4. Criteria/rubrics clearly inform learners as to how they will be assessed on specific assignments, such as online class participation. (164, 175) [C8, C9]

☐ 5. Grading criteria are outlined in the course syllabus and within the assignment or assessment itself. (161) [C8]

☐ 6. Criteria and procedures for peer review and evaluation are clear. (157) [C8]

B.8 Feedback

☐ 1. Teacher, peer-to-peer, guest, and automated feedback clarifies, amplifies, and extends the topic. (146, 157) [C7, C8]

☐ 2. Teacher feedback is provided in a timely fashion. (121, 154) [C6, C8]

☐ 3. Students can work through a practice exercise until they reach a correct or acceptable result. (121) [C8]

☐ 4. Students know when and how they will receive feedback from instructors. (159) [C8]

☐ 5. Self-correcting and/or self-assessment activities are used throughout the course to enable learners to vary the pace of their learning as is appropriate to the subject matter. (122, 157) [C6, C8]

B.9 Evaluation and Grading

☐ 1. All graded activities are listed upfront in the syllabus. (181, 187) [C9]

☐ 3. The manner of submission for graded assignments is clear. (181) [C9]

☐ 4. Due dates for submissions are clear. (181) [C9]

☐ 5. The relationship between graded elements and the final grade is clear. (159) [C8]

☐ 6. Consequences of missed deadlines and insufficient class participation are clearly stated and fair. (181) [C9]

☐ 7. Class participation/discussion should account for 10–30 percent of the final grade. (164) [C8]

☐ 8. Students can easily track their progress. (161) [C8]

☐ 9. The consequences of plagiarism, cheating, and failure to properly cite copyrighted material are emphasized. (133, 181) [C7, C9]

☐ 10. Graded elements are clearly distinguished from those that are ungraded. (159) [C8]

☐ 11. Graded assignments are varied (e.g. special projects, reflective assignments, research papers, case studies, presentations, group work, etc.). (154) [C8]

B.10 | B.10 Ease of Access

☐ 1. Correct, working links are provided to course materials and resources. (132) [C7]

☐ 2. Resource material is accessible to all students in commonly used formats. (147) [C7]

☐ 3. The format of media should be specified. (138) [C7]

☐ 4. Audio and video material appearing within a lesson should be brief. (140) [C7]

☐ 5. Course material is portable (e.g. text can be downloaded or printed out, material is well designed for handheld devices). (74, 147) [C4, C7]

☐ 6. Contact information to advisors and technical help is provided in the syllabus. (177) [C9]

☐ 7. Cross-referencing and links to items in other parts of the course are provided. (147) [C7]

References

ALTEC (2008) Rubistar: What is a rubric? Retrieved from: http://rubistar. 4teachers.org/index.php?screen=WhatIs&module=Rubistar.

Bloom, B.S. (Ed.) (1956) *Taxonomy of Educational Objectives: The Classification of Educational Goals. Handbook I: Cognitive Domain*. New York: Longman.

Boulton, M. (2007) Whitespace. Retrieved from: www.alistapart.com/ articles/whitespace.

Brown, T. (2003) Screen typefaces. Retrieved from: http://adminstaff. vassar.edu/tibrown/thesis/screenfaces.html.

Chickering, A.W. & Gamson, Z.F. (1987) Seven principles for good practice in undergraduate education. *The American Association for Higher Education Bulletin*, March: 3–7.

Conrad, R. & Donaldson, J. (2004) *Engaging the Online Learner*. San Francisco, CA: Jossey-Bass.

Dewey, J. (1938) *Experience and Education*. New York: Free Press.

Edelson, D.C. & Reiser, B.J. (2006) Making authentic practices accessible to learners: Design challenges and strategies. In R. K. Sawyer (Ed.), *The Cambridge Handbook of the Learning Sciences* (pp. 335–354). Cambridge: Cambridge University Press.

Educause (2010) Seven things you should know about assessing online team-based learning. Retrieved from: www.educause.edu/ELI/ELI Resources/7ThingsYouShouldKnowAboutAsses/210831.

Edutopia (1997) Big thinkers: Howard Gardner on multiple intelligences. Retrieved from: www.edutopia.org/multiple-intelligences-howard-gardner-video.

Gardner, H. (1993) *Frames of Mind: The Theory of Multiple Intelligences*. New York: Basic Books.

Hattie, J. & Yates, G.C.R. (2014) *Visible Learning and the Science of How We Learn*. New York: Routledge.

Horton, S. (2006) Design simply. Universal usability: A universal design approach to Web usability. Retrieved from: www.universal usability.com.

References

Lamb, B. (2004) Wide open spaces: Wikis ready or not. *EDUCAUSE Review*, September–October: 36–48.

Lidwell, W., Holden, K., & Butler, J. (2003) *Universal Principles of Design: 125 Ways to Influence Perception, Increase Appeal, Make Better Design Decisions, and Teach through Design*. Beverly, MA: Rockport Publishers.

Lynch, P.J. & Horton, S. (2006) Access by design: Design simply. Retrieved from: http://universalusability.com/access_by_design/fundamentals/simply.html.

Lynch, P.J. & Horton, S. (2009) *Web Style Guide* (3rd ed.). New Haven, CT: Yale University Press.

Lynch, P.J. & Horton, S. (2011) Web style guide online: Typography. Retrieved from: www.webstyleguide.com/wsg3/8-typography/index.html.

Madden, D. (1999) 17 elements of good online courses. Retrieved from: http://honolulu.hawaii.edu/intranet/committees/FacDevCom/guidebk/online/web-elem.htm.

Maeda, J. (2006) *Laws of Simplicity*. Cambridge, MA: MIT Press.

Mayer, R.E. (2001) *Multimedia Learning*. New York: Cambridge University Press.

Mayer, R.E. (2005) *The Cambridge Handbook of Multimedia Learning*. New York: Cambridge University Press.

Medina, J. (2014) *Brain Rules*. Seattle, WA: Pear Press.

Motive Guides (2008) Web typography. Retrieved from: www.motive.co.nz/guides/typography/webfonts.php.

Orwell, G. (1946) *Politics and the English Language*. London: Horizon.

Palloff, R.M. & Pratt, K. (2005) *Collaborating Online: Learning Together in Community*. San Francisco, CA: Jossey-Bass.

Palloff, R.M. & Pratt, K. (2007) *Building Online Learning Communities*. San Francisco, CA: Jossey-Bass.

Prensky, M. (2001) Digital natives, digital immigrants. *On the Horizon*, 9(5).

Quality Matters (2013) Inter-institutional quality assurance in online learning. Retrieved from: www.qualitymatters.org.

Quintana, C., Shin, N., Norris, C., & Soloway, E. (2006) Learner-centered design: Reflections on the past and directions for the future. In R.K. Sawyer (Ed.), *The Cambridge Handbook of the Learning Sciences* (pp. 119–134). Cambridge: Cambridge University Press.

References

Reeves, T. (2006) How do you know they are learning? The importance of alignment in higher education. *International Journal of Learning Technology*, 2(4): 294–309.

Salmon, G. (2002) *E-tivities: The Key to Active Online Learning*. New York: Routledge.

Scardamalia, M. & Bereiter, C. (1991) Higher levels of agency for children in knowledge-building: A challenge for the design of new knowledge media. *The Journal of the Learning Sciences*, 1(1): 37–68.

Shaul, M. (2007) Assessing online discussion forum participation. *The International Journal of Information and Communication Technology Education*, 3: 39–46.

Sosulski, K. & Bongiovanni, T. (2013) *The Savvy Student's Guide to Online Learning*. New York: Routledge.

Stein, J. & Graham, C. (2014) *Essentials for Blended Learning: A Standards-Based Guide*, New York: Routledge.

Strunk, W., Jr. (1918) *The Elements of Style*. Ithaca, NY: W.P. Humphrey.

Strunk, W., Jr. & White, E.B. (1979) *The Elements of Style* (3rd ed.). New York: Macmillan.

Zeinstejer, R. (2008) The wiki revolution: A challenge to traditional education. *TESL-EJ*, 4: 1–8.

Index

Note: Pages numbers in *italics* refer to figures and tables